PUFFIN BOOKS
GURU NANAK

When computers hit the scene, life changed for Sreelata Menon. The Internet introduced her to a whole new way of writing and working. A Masters in History, she was with the *Onlooker* and *World Trade Magazine* before teaching History to undergraduates and doing a stint in an advertising agency. Now working from home, she is a widely-travelled freelance writer who enjoys writing on all kinds of topics.

She writes weekly blogs on freelance writing and content for a variety of websites. She is the author of *Freelance Writing for the Newbie Writer*, which has been released to rave reviews. Married to a civil servant, she has two grown-up sons and now keeps flitting between Delhi and Bangalore.

With my Compliments
Sreelata

323

Other books in the *Puffin Lives* series

GURU

Nanak

THE ENLIGHTENED MASTER

SREELATA MENON

PUFFIN BOOKS

PUFFIN BOOKS
Published by the Penguin Group
Penguin Books India Pvt. Ltd, 11 Community Centre, Panchsheel Park,
New Delhi 110 017, India
Penguin Group (USA) Inc., 375 Hudson Street, New York, New York 10014,
USA
Penguin Group (Canada), 90 Eglinton Avenue East, Suite 700, Toronto,
Ontario, M4P 2Y3, Canada (a division of Pearson Penguin Canada Inc.)
Penguin Books Ltd, 80 Strand, London WC2R 0RL, England
Penguin Ireland, 25 St. Stephen's Green, Dublin 2, Ireland (a division of
Penguin Books Ltd)
Penguin Group (Australia), 250 Camberwell Road, Camberwell, Victoria
3124, Australia (a division of Pearson Australia Group Pty Ltd)
Penguin Group (NZ), 67 Apollo Drive, Rosedale, Auckland 0632,
New Zealand (a division of Pearson New Zealand Ltd)
Penguin Group (South Africa) (Pty) Ltd, 24 Sturdee Avenue, Rosebank,
Johannesburg 2196, South Africa

Penguin Books Ltd, Registered Offices: 80 Strand, London WC2R 0RL,
England

First published in Puffin by Penguin Books India 2011

Copyright © Sreelata Menon 2011

All rights reserved

10 9 8 7 6 5 4 3 2 1

ISBN 9780143331902

Typeset in Bembo by Eleven Arts, Delhi
Printed at Replika Press Pvt. Ltd, Sonepat

When Guru Nanak appeared in this world
The mists lifted, there was light everywhere
Like, with the rising of the sun
Stars hide and darkness retreats,
Like, at the roaring of a lion
The deer flee . . .

Var-1, 27 Bhai Gurdas
(From *The Book of Nanak* by Navtej Sarna)

Contents

1   A Mystery

There was chaos on the banks of the river Bein.

The governor, Daulat Khan Lodhi, himself was supervising the dragging of the river while the entire town of Sultanpur Lodhi was in an uproar. People hung around in little clusters while others darted about agitatedly.

'Have you seen him, have you found him?' they asked each other.

Early that morning, just before the break of dawn, a young man who regularly bathed in the waters of the little rivulet had gone missing. It was his custom to bathe and then sit in meditation under a *ber* tree for a while—every day—before he embarked upon his daily chores.

But that particular morning, his best friend and attendant Mardana waited for him in vain. He hadn't come out of the river like he usually did, nor was he to be found anywhere. In panic Mardana had begun combing the river banks. So did other friends of the young man.

Soon search parties were organized and the entire town began to look for this man who was very popular. A dreamer no doubt and a little withdrawn, but one who nevertheless had a pleasing manner that appealed to all.

'Aren't those his clothes?' asked someone when they found his clothes and shoes on the bank where he had apparently left them before wading into the river. 'Yes they are,' agreed another. And despair spread like wildfire among the crowd of searchers. 'He must have drowned,' they concluded sadly, 'and his body carried away by the currents.' Shaking their heads in sorrowful disbelief, they began to disperse.

The river Bein that flowed through the ancient city of Sultanpur Lodhi in the Punjab in the late 1490s was a perfect place for a dip and a swim, while its banks were ideal for those who wanted to meditate and pray. Since nobody could accept the fact that this young man could without a word or cry disappear after a normal routine bath, they believed they would find him sooner than later. But the fishing nets too threw up no answers, nor the divers who searched the length and breadth of the river. Yet, despite ebbing hopes, they kept looking for him everywhere.

Bathed in gloom the city wore a dismal look. As day gave way to night only one person remained convinced that he would turn up unscathed, alive and smiling. That one person was the young man's doting sister. 'Don't despair,' Nanaki told her brother's wife and children. 'Don't cry; I am sure he is all right. He will be back. He will.'

Three anxious days passed. So did three sleepless nights. And as all hope was giving way to despair and anguish, the young man reappeared just as suddenly as he had disappeared. Exactly as his sister had predicted.

He appeared at a spot upstream about 2 kilometres away from where he had vanished. Everyone flocked around him joyously. 'Where have you been?' they asked. 'We thought you had drowned. Why did you vanish?'

He looked at everyone silently and thoughtfully but gave no answer. Then after a day of complete silence, on the fourth day, a day after his return, he proclaimed, *'There is no Hindu and there is no Musalman. There is only one God and all are equal before Him.'*

While everyone looked on in shock, wondering if he had suddenly gone insane, this man, with that one prophetic announcement, laid the foundation of a new faith based on love, equality among all men and devotion to one God.

His name?

Nanak. Meaning brother of Nanaki. Guru Nanak, as he was soon to be known the world over, had delivered on that fateful day the first words that were to form the core of a creed that would span centuries and spread over continents.

He had just founded the world's youngest religion 'Sikhism'; a religion that was to become the fifth largest religion in the world after Christianity, Islam, Hinduism and Buddhism.

But the question was, where had he been? Where had he gone? Where had he disappeared for those three days?

The City of Sultanpur Lodhi

In the 1490s, the ancient city of Sultanpur Lodhi through which the rivulet Kali Bein flowed, was situated strategically at the confluence of the rivers Beas and Sutlej. It was an important commercial hub on the Lahore–Delhi trade route. Known as Sarwmanpur in the first century, it had been a thriving Buddhist centre of learning till sacked and destroyed by Mahmud of Ghazni in the 12th century. Subsequently revived and renamed after Sultan Khan Lodhi, one of the sons of the then ruler of Punjab Nawab Wali Muhammad Khan, it was at that point in time a bustling little town famous not only for its commerce but also for its beautiful royal gardens and educational cum religious institutions. Many of the later Mughal princes, including Aurangzeb, are said to have studied there. Ruins of the era can still be found. It is today a part of Punjab in the district of Kapurthala.

Kali Bein by virtue of its significance in Sikh history is one of the more important rivers in the Punjab or the land of five rivers.160 miles long, it originates near the city of Hoshiarpur then flows through the towns of Kapurthala and Sultanpur Lodhi till it merges with the river Sutlej, one of the five rivers in Punjab, near a place called Hari ke Patan. Called Kali (black) Bein due to the black reflection of the minerals in it, the Kali Bein finds mention even in *Ain-e-Akbari*, the third volume of the

Akbarnama, a 16th century Persian document written by Akbar's prime minister Abul Fazl that details the administration, governance and life under Emperor Akbar. Reduced to a dirty narrow channel by the 20th century, the Kali Bein has been revived and given a new lease of life in 2000 by a group of Sikh devotees who spent almost six years cleaning and desilting the once glorious waters. The Gurdwara Ber Sahib exists even today by the side of the old ber tree under which Guru Nanak was believed to have meditated.

2 💮 India in the 15th Century

India in the 15th century was not very different from the India of the 21st century as far as conflict and hostilities were concerned. There was strife and war everywhere just as there is even today. Again, like today, it was also a period of social unrest and religious disharmony. And life for the people in Punjab was particularly tough. Rulers came and went. While they brought oppression and repression with them when they came, they went leaving behind death and destruction.

Starting with Qutub-ud-in-Aibek's Slave dynasty, India was ruled by a succession of dynasties right from the 12th century. The Slave dynasty was in turn followed by the Khiljis, the Tughlaks, the Sayyids and finally the Lodhis of the Delhi Sultanate.

The Sultanate controlled most of India from Bengal in the east to the Deccan in the south till they (the Lodhis) were overthrown by Babur who established the Mughal Empire. This period saw a lot of instability and insurgency with some small periods of peace in between, depending on the personality of the ruler.

Conditions were not only hard and unhappy for all Hindus but, strange as it may seem, it was no better for the Muslims as well, especially the poor. Power was concentrated in the hands of the invaders, almost all of whom were Sunni Muslims and generally Afghans. There wasn't much love lost between the rulers and the ruled as they generally tended to look down upon the local people. They were not only cruel and unkind but were religious fanatics as well. Though in comparison to his predecessors he was considerably less harsh and much kinder, Sikander Lodhi (1488–1518) who ruled Delhi was a zealous bigot, intolerant of other religions, and he levied the much hated 'Jizya' tax on all non-Muslims.

Even without the 'Jizya', life for the Hindus under these rulers was a miserable and pitiful affair. Religious persecution, too, was almost a daily affair. In fact, the Hindus themselves were a lot to blame for their miserable condition. They made their own situation considerably worse by following a rigid caste system that not only aggravated their misery but also created its own set of problems. They also treated their women shamefully. But it must also be said that the Hindus were not solely to blame for this; there were historical reasons too. Although their fate was worse than slaves and they were forced to follow practices that were quite inhuman, it was also an unfortunate fallout of the various Muslim invasions that kept occurring. Women had to be protected from these marauding raiders and so gradually their freedom got restricted. Then the influence of the Muslim invaders' negative attitude towards women percolated down to the masses, who gradually began to see women as inferior.

In a nutshell, the condition of women during the Middle Ages in India was dismal. Widows were treated like outcastes and selfish Brahmins of the priestly class dictated all social practices. Female infanticide or killing of infants was prevalent and child marriages were widespread. Since religion was all important, the priests and the clergy became powerful even among the Muslims.

This meant, in simple terms, that if you needed to please God, you needed to use their services for rituals and ceremonies. So the Brahmin priests and the mullahs were the ones who got to decide if rituals and ceremonies were required—more rituals and ceremonies meant more money in their pockets. Many amongst them were not only greedy and selfish but also good at fooling the innocent into believing that they could reach God only through them. Apart from them, there were sadhus, yogis and sanyasis who roamed the countryside conning the gullible with black magic and superstition.

It is in this environment where society was segregated along lines of religion, caste and creed that young Guru Nanak had grown up. It was a society that thrived on religious hate and divisive inequality; a society that lived in great disharmony.

Yet such was Nanak's popularity that despite their own tribulations, the question uppermost on everyone's mind when he went missing and then reappeared was where and why he had disappeared.

Jizya

Jizya was a tax imposed in all Muslim countries on those who were not prepared to embrace Islam but wanted to practise their own religion. It guaranteed them the state's protection in case of an attack by invaders. It was paid by all Jews and Christians in lieu of military service and was levied on the Hindus for the first time in India around the 11th century CE when Muslims began their forays into the country. It was hugely hated and was regarded as a forced weapon of conversion and a mark of humiliation by a population already overburdened by other Muslim atrocities. It was prevalent as late as the 20th century in Morocco and in Turkey and other Muslim countries like Algeria and Tunisia till recently.

The Punjab before the Lodhis

The Punjab of the 15th century consisted of the Greater Punjab that included large areas of West Pakistan and north-west India. Rich and fertile due to its five river and its proximity to Afghanistan and Baluchistan, it attracted constant invasions west of its borders. Much before these invasions, it was home to the Indus Valley civilization and the Aryans, as well as the Persians, the Greeks and the white Huns. The white Huns were followed by the Arabs. The Slave dynasty set the ball rolling for the Muslim occupation of India and the rule of the Lodhis.

3   A Mystical Experience

So the question uppermost on everyone's mind was, where had Nanak been those three days? Nobody really knows. Historical facts are few and anecdotal narratives are many with regard to Guru Nanak's life. What we know about his life and times is from Nanak's own writings and poems set to music, and the anecdotal biographies called Janamsakhis by later Gurus. But they don't contain many personal details. While there is some confusion regarding what really happened when he disappeared, there is hardly any doubt about the fact that it did happen.

Some accounts speak about his disappearance into a forest nearby while others say that when he dived into the river he was led into the Kingdom of God where he had some kind of a mystical experience. Legend has it that God Himself appeared and spoke to him. And thus enlightened, he came back to spread the word of God.

How much of this is actual fact and how much is embellishment we have no idea, but suffice to say that all accounts are unanimous in the belief that he did disappear for three days near the river and when he appeared he was a different man—an enlightened one. He himself has said in verse that he had received divine instructions to go out among the people and teach them the path of love and tolerance; of honesty and truthfulness; of service and mercy; and that there is only one God. These verses form the first stanza of what is now known as the 'Japji' in the Guru Granth Sahib, the holy book of the Sikhs.

It is a known fact that Nanak, even as a boy, was far ahead of his times in his thinking. The prevailing political conditions around him, along with the misery brought on by blind faith and meaningless rituals, probably set him thinking about ways and means of breaking free and changing people's way of thinking.

Whenever there are harsh, unequal living conditions or sustained persecution of any kind—as is happening all over the world even today—people begin to question and rebel. And history also tells us that whenever this is combined with political peace or weak governance, there is also a surge in the freedom of thought and expression within the country. Poets and thinkers pop up unafraid to express their views. Saints and religious leaders are born prepared to lead from the front. When that happens, there is a revolution of sorts particularly if the anger is against the ruling power.

Why do you suppose the French (1789) and the American (1783) revolutions took place, and the Russian (1917)? The French and the Russians wanted to overthrow their ineffective and selfish monarchies while the Americans sought liberty from their equally selfish mother country Britain. And if the anger is against the stranglehold of religion then it gives rise to the demand for a 'Reformation' of the church, like it did in Germany in 1517 when a group of reformers led by Martin Luther revolted against the corrupt practices of the Catholic Church.

So it was during the Lodhi rule. Amidst all the religious instability it also witnessed a semblance of political calm for a while. This allowed people to think and question existing norms, which in turn gave rise to new ideas. Similarly, though not on scales as large as those of the revolutions around the world but in a more modest and definitely non-violent way, people in medieval India started to feel rebellious and hostile towards the kind of religion propagated by the priestly class. It created among them a school of thinkers and non-believers who were not scared to rebel. They began to question the authority of the Brahmins, the Ulemas and the Qazis. This gave momentum to the Sufi movement among the Muslims in the north and the Bhakti movement among the Hindus across the country.

People like Baba Farid, Kabir and many others began influencing people into breaking away from the clutches of godmen and superstition. They began denouncing rituals and ceremonies and decrying the caste system. They also began promoting a direct personal link to a single God. They sang about a God who loved and did not punish. A God who did not need the intervention of Brahmins or Ulemas to bless the faithful. A God before whom all were equal. And a God who did not have to be feared. What they were doing was actually effecting a revolution, a kind of reformation in the way society thought of God.

So it happened that young Guru Nanak began to preach and convert, to blaze a new trail as foretold by Pandit Hardyal, the village astrologer, way back in 1469 when he had been called to cast a little boy's horoscope.

The Sufi and Bhakti movements

Both existed in India before Sikhism and are generally considered to be very similar. Sufism is an offshoot of Islam. It emphasizes the importance of one God and the need to remember him constantly through personal interaction and expressions of love while searching for truth. There were four important orders of Sufis in India during the 15th century. Named after the Sufi leaders they followed, they were the Chishtis, Qadiris, Suhrawardis and Naqshbandis. They had no uniform doctrine nor were they a defined sect. Their beliefs were purely based on the Koran and the Hadith which revolved round the life and practices of the Prophet. They believed singing and dancing was one definite way of getting to God. They advocated tolerance and piety and believed in the equality of all men.

The Bhakti movement too, though rooted in Hinduism, spread the belief that there was only one God and that a more direct personal link to Him could be achieved without middlemen and by singing devotional songs in praise of Him. They too denounced the caste system and the blind ritualism that was prevalent. Ramanujam in the south and Ramanand in the north were the main propounders of the underlying philosophy of this movement, while men like Kabir, a Muslim weaver, and Ravidas, a cobbler, tried to forge a common bond with God through songs and spiritual verses in praise of a single God.

While the Sufi traditions of the movement still linger on in many countries including India, the Bhakti movement appears to have gradually petered out.

4   The Beginnings

The story of Guru Nanak begins in the little village of Talwandi near Lahore, now in Pakistan.

'It is a boy!' exclaimed Daulatan, the midwife, holding the baby aloft. 'A perfect baby boy.' 'Let me see, let me see,' cried an excited Nanaki, running in to see her little brother while his father Mehta Kalu sat back in pride. 'A boy,' he muttered to himself looking pleased. Good. A pair of able hands, he must have thought, to help him in his business. He was the village chief accountant after all, and a propertied man. He was sure he could do with some help in later years. 'Can I hold him now?' asked his mother Tripta Devi, exhausted after her efforts to bring her son into the world.

'A beautiful child,' intoned the astrologer as he pored over his astrological calculations, 'meant for greatness, one whose name and fame will spread across the world.' Mehta Kalu and his wife were devout Hindus of the Bedi clan who were Khatris by caste. As was the custom among all upper-caste Hindus, a horoscope for a newborn was a must. When Hardyal Pandit made his predictions about their son, the parents, though not quite sure what he meant, were happy all the same. And since the little girl who kept looking so adoringly at her little brother was called Nanaki, they decided to name him Nanak. It was the 15th of April and the year 1469.

Everyone who was present there that day was amazed at the sheer radiance on the baby's face. Daulatan the midwife, it is said, was prepared to swear that the whole room took on the same glow, as if the newborn had the sparkle of a star. She was also convinced that the newborn even chuckled at birth; like someone who knew something that others did not.

Nanak was a self-contained little boy. Quiet and contemplative, he liked going off on his own. In the joint family that he grew up, his best friend and confidant was his sister Nanaki. Five years older, she not only assisted her mother at home but also helped take care of him. She herself was a lovely child, kind and caring, and she adored Nanak. As far as she was concerned Nanak could do no wrong. It was she who first realized very early in life that there was something quite exceptional about him.

He was just four years old when he began showing a spiritual bent of mind. While playing with the children of the village, one day he asked them to gather around. 'Let's chant the name of God,' he said and led the singing. His voice soared high and true. The fervour with which he sang had everyone, including Rai Bular, the chief of Talwandi, shake their heads in disbelief and admiration. This soon became a regular feature. The Hindus of the village were amazed and the Muslims were astonished. Both communities believed that he was destined for divinity.

When he was about seven, Mehta Kalu decided that while God and spirituality were all fine, what the boy needed was some sound education. 'Come Nanak,' he said, 'I think it's time you started school.' A good education, he must have thought, would keep the boy from getting into mischief, spiritual or otherwise!

And so off he was sent to the village school where the local pandit doubled up as a teacher. No sooner had Pandit Gopal started with the Devnagari alphabet than Nanak composed an acrostic—a poem in which the letters of the lines spell out a message—with all the thirty-five letters of the alphabet on his Patti. Pattis were wooden tablets on which a kind of liquid chalk was used to write. They were widely used in the medieval ages.

Nanak also told him that each letter stood for God the creator, and existed only to praise his creation and was actually useless otherwise. The amazed teacher knew that this was no ordinary child. It was soon evident that Nanak knew more than his teacher. He even composed a poem for his teacher describing what true learning should be and how it should revolve round the name of God and His thoughts.

So Pandit Gopal sent him off to Pandit Brijlal who was spiritually inclined and a brilliant Sanskrit teacher. However, even the Sanskrit classics he was taught were easy for Nanak and he soon outdistanced his master.

Now, with both the pandits having failed to hold his attentions, Nanak's father was at his wits' end as to how to keep him occupied and prevent him from wandering off on his own as he was so often wont to do. He was also found increasingly in the company of sadhus and saints. All this did not please his parents at all.

It was then decided to let him study Persian under the Muslim Maulvi of Talwandi. Since Persian was the language of administration, his father and the village chief Rai Bular believed that it would come in useful when he was old enough to take up a job, perhaps as the village accountant. But here again he was soon composing poems in perfect Persian about the temporary nature of man's existence in the world. The stunned Maulvi realized he too had nothing to offer that the boy didn't know already. Nanak was then just nine years old.

Nanak continued to amaze everyone with his spiritual knowledge all through his growing years. He constantly astonished his teachers and his family with his tremendous grasp of spirituality by composing spiritual hymns and songs. His command over the language too was remarkable even at that tender age.

In fact when he was about eleven, on the day of his Upanayanam or janeu when the priest, amidst all the chanting mantras and many grandly attired relatives and friends gathered there, was about to put the sacred thread around him, Nanak told him 'Stop,' and asked: 'What use is this thread? Why do I need to wear it?' When the priest told him that the sacred cotton thread was a symbol of his high birth and lineage, he came up with this gem:

> *Out of the cotton of compassion*
> *Spin the thread of contentment*
> *Tie knots of continence; give it the twist of truth.*
> *Make such a sacred thread for the mind (soul)*
> *Such a thread once worn will never break*
> *Nor get soiled, burnt or lost*
> *The man who weareth such a thread is blessed.*
> (From *The Great Humanist Guru Nanak*
> by Raja D. Singh and J. Singh)

He also shocked the congregation by refusing to wear it, saying it was no more sacred than the cotton from which it was spun; that it would decay, break and would be left behind when the wearer died. On the other hand, he believed that a life lived with compassion, contentment and truth were the true symbols of a high lineage, and so he told the priest, 'If you have one such thread, put it on me.' Despite their dismay, those gathered felt there was indeed some truth in what he had just said.

Nanak didn't stop there. He further went on to ask the priest in simple words:

> *Thou buyest a thread for a pice*
> *And seated in a plastered square,*
> *Puteth it around the neck of others*

Claiming an inheritance of holiness
Thy thread helps neither here nor here after.
(From *The Great Humanist Guru Nanak*
by Raja D. Singh and J. Singh)

'And so how holy or helpful could it really be when it was of no use then or after death?'

It is evident that even at that age Nanak was able to perceive the difference between empty symbolism and actual spirituality. He was also very confident of the truth of his convictions. He was not only questioning the blind faith in ancient rituals but also questioning the holy men who were perpetuating it.

How do we know all this? From time immemorial, history has left its imprints on cave walls, pillars, sculptures and carvings on stone. Guru Nanak left his in the Janamsakhis or stories that have been handed down to us through the centuries.

Guru Purab

Guru Nanak is said to have been born on the full-moon day of 15 April 1469, according to the Hindu lunar based solar calendar. But with changes in calendar fixation, there is some confusion as to whether it was on the full-moon day in April or the month of 'kartik' in October/November. Although several ancient records now indicate April, other compilations show November, and so historians are undecided. But despite this, perhaps in order to maintain a continuity of a tradition that dates back a few centuries, his birthday is today generally celebrated as Guru Purab in October/November.

Talwandi

Originally built by Raja Vairat, Talwandi was named Raipur or Rai Bhoe ki Talwandi after its chieftain Rai Bhoi Bhatti—a Muslim Rajput, who was appointed by the Delhi Sultans. Although it lay right in the path of the marauding invaders who made regular forays into Hindustan from Afghanistan and Central Asia, under Bhatti's son Rai Bular, it was a prosperous little town with several acres of cultivation.

Rai Bular, an ardent admirer of Nanak, gifted him about 20,000 acres of land in and around Talwandi which soon came to be known as Nankana. After Guru Nanak achieved eminence it became famous the world over as Nankana Sahib—the place of his birth. It is now a part of the district of Nankana Sahib in the province of Punjab in Pakistan and is about fifty miles from Lahore. Predominantly Muslim, it however boasts of nine Sikh Gurdwaras. Though it is home to only a few permanent Sikh families, thousands visit during festivals, especially during Guru Purab. Today a bus service runs between Amritsar in India and Nankana Sahib in Pakistan.

5 🌾 The Janamsakhis

Storytelling sessions are a part of our growing-up years. You must have heard tales of Lord Rama's prowess with the bow or Arjuna's bravery. Or about the miracle of the birth of baby Jesus in a barn and how Moses made the seas part. Similarly, stories about the exploits of a young Nanak who sought to change the rigid mindset of adults through examples, and how he went on in later life to prove his point through miracles—wrought by the power of prayer—have been handed down from generation to generation.

Many of these stories first came to light from old texts found scattered in various Gurdwaras or Sikh places of worship around the world. They were essentially the same stories but written in different styles with many additions and deletions.

There were many such texts. Yet the one considered most authentic was composed by Bhai Gurdas, who was the nephew of the third Guru—Guru Amar Das. It was written about eighty years after Guru Nanak died. Bhai Gurdas was a contemporary of a certain Bhai Buddha who had known Guru Nanak as a child.

Now this is not unusual. Almost all great men including Jesus Christ have had their lives written about much after their deaths. The only exception to the rule being perhaps Lord Rama who heard about the trials and tribulations of his own life from his two estranged sons, Luv and Kush. So apart from the story of Rama, almost all biographical narratives have been composed much after the death of the person they are writing about. And it is usually done by one or the other of his followers, like Bhai Gurdas who composed his 39 vars in praise of Guru Nanak. It was in the nature of a tribute to him, but only a few, especially the first twenty to twenty-five stanzas in it, speak about Guru Nanak's personal life. Overall it is mostly about his teachings. It is this that gives us our first authentic but brief account of Guru Nanak's life. Similar stories like these and others—which include anecdotes and happenings that occurred during the life of Guru Nanak and after—that have survived orally for many years began to be compiled and written by various subsequent followers and later Gurus. These collections of stories and anecdotes came to be known as Janamsakhis: 'Janam' meaning birth or life, and 'sakhi' meaning stories.

These Birth Stories or Janamsakhis generally belong to the 17th-19th centuries. They record Nanak's miracles, his teachings and without doubt support his divinity. They are in Sant Basha and Punjabi—the dialect and language of those times—but the script is Gurmukhi.

They are full of drama and colour and contain many, perhaps exaggerated, descriptive details. Although they rarely contain any mention of the time, place or date, they do tell us a lot about the conditions existing at the time. Every story carries a moral lesson and every tale draws our attention to one or the other of Guru Nanak's teachings.

A few years ago, an auction of Indian antiques in London caused much consternation among the Sikh community. The *Amritsar Times* even came out with a special news report about the event. What was on sale was a page from one of the Janamsakhis which is, as the newspaper said, a piece of Punjab's cultural heritage and Sikh history. The Janamsakhi is obviously no ordinary antique to the Sikhs. It is a link to their past, their very existence. It is our only window into the life and times of Guru Nanak.

Even though there are many Janamsakhis, and scholars and subsequent historians doubt their authenticity, it is an accepted fact that without the Janamsakhis our knowledge about Guru Nanak's life and those of his followers would be sketchy if not incomplete.

It is true that they were composed much after the death of Guru Nanak by faithful followers. It is also true that they are vague as far as Guru Nanak's personal details are concerned. And it cannot also be denied that many historians believe they are at times coloured or influenced by the writer's own thoughts and beliefs; that they sometimes appear contradictory to each other or even seem unreliable. Yet these stories have immense value for they are the only written records that throw light on Guru Nanak's life. What had till then been handed down orally by word of mouth based on legend and tradition was for the first time given a collective narrative form in verse and put down in writing by those who could.

Many scholars like Seva Ram Singh, Ernest Trumpp, M.A. Macauliffe and Bhai Vir Singh have spent most of their lives deciphering and sifting through these Janamsakhis to research, translate and produce much of what we know today. Since there are several Janamsakhis, there are also some whose authorship is suspect or even unknown.

In fact the India Office library in London has a manuscript titled accession number B-40 still lying with them. It is a Janamsakhi written in 1773 and is perhaps the oldest existing manuscript in the Punjabi language. This Janamsakhi has in it fifty-seven exquisite paintings done in true Sikh tradition. It was apparently purchased from a Muslim by the library for ten pounds in 1907.

For those who are interested in checking them out, the Chandigarh Government Museum will be a good place to visit. Many Janamsakhis belonging to the 18th and 19th centuries are preserved carefully there.

It is therefore certain that the Janamsakhis, however spurious some of them might be, are of great importance to us in keeping the story of Guru Nanak alive.

Janamsakhi compilations

There are four broadly accepted traditions of Janamsakhis.

The Bhai Bala Janamsakhi:

Written apparently when many of Guru Nanak's contemporaries were still alive, it is said to have been dictated and taken down in the presence of the second Guru, Guru Angad, by Bhai Bala who was also a contemporary of Guru Nanak. He supposedly accompanied Guru Nanak on his travels and gives us an authoritative account about his life and travels. But today much of it is discounted by historians because the language is inconsistent and it appears to have been tampered with by subsequent writers.

The Puratan Janamsakhi:

Written about eighty years after the death of Guru Nanak, this is believed to be the oldest. It contains (1) The Vilayati Wali Janamsakhi which was discovered and sent to London by one H.T. Colebrooke of the East India Company and (2) The Hafizabad Wali Janamsakhi that was discovered by an acclaimed Sikh scholar, Bhai Gurmukh Singh of Oriental College Lahore in Hafizabad, and sent to M.A. Macauliffe, an ICS member and scholar who was researching and writing on the Sikh religion. Macauliffe's *The Sikh Religion* runs into six volumes and is today considered one of the most authoritative works on Sikhism.

The Meharban Janamsakhi:

Written by Sodhi Meharban (1581–1640), a grandson of the fourth Guru, Guru Ram Das, it appeared to have authenticity till it was found that his father Prithichand had apparently broken away from Sikh traditions and could have been influenced by heretics. It was only discovered in 1940 and has subsequently been deemed hostile despite its well-developed style and prose.

The Bhai Mani Singh Ratnavali:

Written by Bhai Mani Singh, a businessman during the time of Guru Gobind Singh, it is an elaboration of a selection of stories borrowed from earlier Janamsakhis. In particular it borrows from Bhai Gurdas' first vars written about eighty years after Guru Nanak's death as also some from the Bhai Bala Janamsakhi. Bhai Mani Singh's authorship, however, has been questioned by later scholars.

In 1926 another distinguished Sikh, Bhai Vir Singh, compiled stories from various Janamsakhis including the Vilayati Wali and Hafizabad ones into a composite work and had it published.

6   Glimpses of Divinity

We know from the Janamsakhis that while growing up, Nanak spent most of his free time with various holy men. This greatly disturbed his parents. Mehta Kalu couldn't understand why his son, who appeared to be by all accounts so intelligent, should want to hang around with sadhus and maulvis instead of studying or preparing for a job that would be profitable. Why can't he be more responsible? he wondered. He was not to know that Nanak only hung around with these holy men to satisfy his immense curiosity. Nanak, like any child, was taken up by the wonders of nature. But unlike most other children he was not prepared to merely accept the fact that they were just there. He was intrigued. He was amazed by the beauty of nature and he felt a need to find out who created it and how.

He wasn't getting any answers from people he knew, so he had taken to discussing it with whoever he thought could help him understand. And if they happened to be holy men and sadhus who had renounced the world, all the better. So he peppered them with inquisitive questions not only about why they had taken sanyas, but also if they had found what they were looking for. He continued to ask:

Who made night and day
The days of the week, the seasons?
Who made the breezes blow, the waters flow
And the fires, the lower regions?
He who made them made the earth too.
                    (From *Nanak the Guru* by Mala Dayal)

And not quite satisfied with their answers, he would quietly draw his own conclusions. In the process he was being drawn deeper and deeper into the world of spirituality and God, much to his father's distress.

Added to that, he had also begun to exhibit some glimpses of divinity which were perhaps not apparent to him but to others. These soon began convincing everyone that he was indeed truly blessed.

Rai Bular, for instance, was on his way home one hot day when in the distance he spotted a cobra. It appeared to be motionless, its hood spread as if protecting something. This was unusual because cobras as we all know are poisonous snakes and they spread their hoods only when they are in an attack mode. As he approached the snake, Rai Sahib discovered little Nanak all curled up and fast asleep under it. Almost convinced that Nanak had been bitten, he was about to raise a hue and cry when the cobra slithered away quietly and Nanak woke up. The snake, much to Rai Bular's disbelief, had been actually trying to shade the sleeping boy from the sun's harsh rays and not harm him.

Earlier, on another occasion, when he had found Nanak asleep in the fields, he had noticed that the tree under which he lay was the only one that appeared to have shade, as if in protection of the sleeping boy.

If Rai Bular needed any more confirmation about the divinity of the child in their midst, he was to get it again soon enough when Mehta Kalu, tired of having his son do nothing but wander around in thought, decided to send him off to graze his herd of buffaloes. Nanak, who loved to escape into the fields whenever he could, was thrilled at the prospect. It meant he would be free to contemplate undisturbed. But unfortunately for Nanak, this time when he was as usual lost in thought, his cattle went on a rampage in a neighbouring field.

The owner, seeing his devastated crops, lost no time in complaining to Rai Bular. He wanted compensation for his ruined crops. So Rai Bular sent his men to check out the damage. But to their surprise, the men, including the owner, found all the crops in full bloom and not a single one damaged! This, more than anything else, was enough to convince Rai Bular that he had indeed witnessed some kind of a godly phenomenon. And like the doting Nanaki, Rai Bular too was now more than convinced about the extraordinary powers of the child.

Mehta Kalu, however, was not. He wasn't ready to give up on his ideas of what he wanted his son to be. He was determined that like all other boys, his son too should earn a living, if not as a farmer or a grazer, then at least as a shopkeeper or a trader. So he sent him off with about twenty-one mohurs or silver coins to do some business and turn a profit. Nanak spent it all on food and groceries for a group of unfed, hungry sadhus he happened to come across on the way. When an angry Mehta asked him sarcastically how much profit he had made, his son calmly replied that the profit was in the giving and it was as good a bargain as any, for 'money cannot accompany man, can it, when he dies?' His father had no answer.

And thus Nanak continued unfazed to do his own thing.

The last straw as far as his father was concerned was when one day Nanak took to his bed and wouldn't eat or drink for many days despite his mother's pleas. The doctor was called and when he was being examined, a listless Nanak told him that no medicine could cure him as the 'sickness is in my heart . . . in my soul and the pain can only be cured by the creator, the one true God because for a brief moment I had forgotten Him.' The physician went away shaking his head, convinced that there was physically nothing wrong that Nanak couldn't cure himself.

Often during his adolescence Nanak increasingly, due to his preoccupied nature and lack of direction, ran foul of his father. Every time it was his sister Nanaki who pacified both parties and took his side. For didn't she know in her heart that he was meant for greater things, and that he was like no other ordinary boy? His father, helpless in the face of all this, began to wonder rather reluctantly if perhaps Nanaki and Rai Bular were right after all, that Nanak was unlike most other boys. Nanak was soon to prove them all right.

Nanaki, sadly for Nanak, was soon married off to Jairam, a revenue official in the office of the governor of Lahore, Daulat Khan Lodhi, and sent to Sultanpur which was at a considerable distance from Talwandi. Seeing the boy mope around following his sister's departure, his parents decided to get him married too. He was just twelve when he was married to a girl called Sulakhani from the village of Palihoke Randhawa near the town of Batala. She was to later—when they grew up and came of age—bear him two sons: Sri Chand and Lakshmi Das.

Marriage didn't bring about any change in Nanak. After all, they were still children and child marriages were actually just traditional ceremonial contracts between families till the children became adults. So when Nanak continued to seek the company of holy men to engage in endless discussions about the creator, his worried parents wondered whether a stay with his sister and brother-in-law in Sultanpur for a while might do him good.

And so, along he went to Sultanpur where he was soon joined by his childhood friend Mardana. His father felt that Mardana, who was a singer by profession, would keep an eye on Nanak. Mardana was to become his best friend and attendant for life.

Nanaki was overjoyed to see Nanak, and he too was happy to be with his sister. She understood and loved him for who he was. Her husband, who too was fond of Nanak, fixed him up as a storekeeper in Daulat Khan Lodhi's office.

For the first time in many years Nanak appeared to be at peace. He diligently went about his work while following a strict daily routine. He would wake up before dawn, bathe in the nearby river Bein and meditate for a while under a ber tree. Thereafter he and Mardana would sing his compositions—hymns and songs—in praise of God. He would then go to work in the store. He was so meticulous in his accounts that Daulat Khan Lodhi soon grew fond of him. In the evening, after work, he would be found once again with Mardana, singing his hymns. A community dinner would follow where everyone would sit and eat together. Caste, creed and religion didn't matter. And gradually the congregation grew larger and larger. Like the Upanayanam incident, he was once again leading by example.

Life at Sultanpur Lodhi thus went by till Nanak suddenly disappeared for those three days and rose from the waters of the Bein declaring, *'There is no Hindu and there is no Musalman. There is only one God and all are equal before Him.'*

Child Marriages

Can you imagine your little sister, all of three or four years old, married? Well, that is what used to happen in Guru Nanak's time. Child marriages were a common practice in medieval India. One of the reasons was to forge alliances with kingdoms; marriage would merge kingdoms or bring peace to warring ones. Secondly, due to the constant Muslim invasions, parents got their little girls married off sometimes even in their cradles to protect them. These girls continued to stay on in their own homes even after marriage or went on long visits to the grooms' homes till they were old enough to start living together, as did Sulakhani and Nanak. So if you were a girl or a boy in the middle ages, chances are that you would be married by the time you reached your tenth birthday!

But even after the middle ages, due to poverty or for lower dowries or to prevent them from eloping with unsuitable boys once they grew up, parents continued to get their little girls married off. They were married off to much older men or sent to their new homes at a tender age when they should be playing and studying. These girls remained uneducated and were usually ill-treated, bearing dozens of children which in turn affected their health. Sadly, this is rampant even in the villages of today's India. The fact is that they are even today being forced into such alliances at an age when they are too young to know their rights. So now laws have been passed to make it illegal for a girl below eighteen and a boy below twenty-one to get married. But the girl child continues to be treated badly and the practice still continues in rural India where ways of thinking has not changed much.

7 No Hindu, No Musalman

When Nanak reappeared declaring that *'there is no Hindu and there is no Musalman . . .'* the crowd who had gathered there to welcome him grew restive. As far as they were concerned, such a statement was a sacrilege to both the Muslims and the Hindus. In a society that was steeped in the caste system and replete with rituals and idols, this was a new thought. It was, as far as they were aware, a blasphemous one too. Since both believed in the superiority of their own religions, how could 'all be equal before God'?

'He has lost his mind,' they decided, but when they found he had not, the Qazi of Sultanpur got annoyed. He wanted the governor to take action against him at once. So Nanak was summoned before the governor and the Qazi at the mosque, when the afternoon prayers were in process. Nanak stood while all others knelt down in prayer.

Admonished by the Qazi as to why he wasn't praying, Nanak asked him, 'Do your prayers consist only of kneeling and bowing?'

'No,' said the Qazi, 'it is merely an outward expression of our humbleness before God.'

'Then tell me,' replied Nanak, 'what is the inward expression?'

'It is the sincerity of the spirit in which the prayer is offered,' replied the Qazi.

'If that is so, then why,' asked Nanak, 'was your mind on your newborn horse and why was the governor thinking about the stable of horses in Kabul he is planning to buy while your bodies were bending and bowing?' Thunderstruck by not only his ability to read their thoughts but also by the truth of his words, the Qazi admitted that his mind had indeed been elsewhere as did the governor.

Nanak then told them that to be a proper Musalman and a true disciple of the Prophet it was necessary to get rid of one's pride and ego and be sincere in thought, belief and action. This message is applicable to everyone.

His message: *You don't become a true Muslim or Hindu by merely mouthing the words of God or by simply going through the motions. There is only one God and He is supreme and all powerful. You need to learn to understand the words of the prayers, believe in them and then repeat them. Only then will our minds be purified.*

In other words, be sincere in whatever you are doing and do it with your whole mind. So just in case you were thinking of that new video game when you should be studying, think again!

On another occasion, right in the heartland of Islam in Mecca, Guru Nanak was asked by the chief priest at the Kaaba whether he was a Muslim from a far-off land. 'Why do you ask?' asked Nanak. 'Because you preach of one God and Muslims too believe in only one God,' answered the Muslim priest.

Nanak replied, 'The Vedas too speak of one God, the supreme God who goes by many names but is one. That would make me a Hindu too, wouldn't it? But if as you say God is one, then how can there be any difference in His followers? If you were a true believer you would know that there can really be no divisions of religion or creed before God. That God sees no one as Hindu or Muslim and that this difference is man-made. It is a difference which is all in the minds of men. In any case there is only one God and I am a man of that God. A God who is eternal, the true creator who dwells everywhere and before whom all are equal, and who recognizes all men who are truthful and carry out good deeds.'

His message: *I am both Hindu and Muslim, or whatever other creed there may be. And so are all men and women. As far as God is concerned there is no difference. God is also neither only Hindu nor only Muslim. His blessing extends to all those who live a life of compassion, truth and piety regardless of faith, religion or creed. He is the Creator, and is hence common to all.*

In other words God is one. He has created all of us. So whether we follow Muhammad or Jesus Christ, Vishnu or Shiva, we are to God all the same. Nobody is inferior or superior to the other, especially in God's eyes.

And that's how it should be amongst us as well, don't you think?

Soon after the incident with the Qazi, Nanak felt the time had come for him to leave Sultanpur. He bade farewell to his tearful family and set out on his travels.

Who is a Muslim?

A person who follows the religion of Islam is a Muslim. He believes in 'Allah' who as the creator is God. All Muslims believe that He is the only one who is worthy of being worshipped. No one else can be worshipped nor do they recognize any other as God. Muhammad is His messenger and is thus the Prophet. A Muslim can be of any country or any race and gender as long as he believes in 'Allah' and lives his life according to the tenets of Islam. The five pillars of Islam are—Proof of Faith known as Kalima, Prayer known as Salat, Almsgiving known as Zakat, Fasting known as Sawm and Pilgrimages known as Haj.

A recent survey (2009) tells us that there are about 1.5 billion Muslims in the world, with the maximum scattered across in countries like Indonesia, Pakistan, Bangladesh, Iran, Turkey, Egypt, Nigeria, Algeria and even China, which has the lowest number while Indonesia has the highest. There are apparently more Muslims in Indonesia than even the Arab countries which only account for about twelve per cent of the world's numbers since not all Arabs are Muslims. Europe and the U.S. too have seen its spread in recent years. India has the fourth largest number of Muslims after Pakistan and Bangladesh, which rank second and third to Indonesia's first. While one fourth of the world's total population today is Muslim, sixty per cent of its Muslims live in Asia.

Who is a Hindu?

A person who follows the Vedas and lives by the rules of Dharma (ethics and duties) is by definition a Hindu. The four Vedas and by extension the Upanishads, the Smritis, Puranas, Bhagavad Gita etc. are generally what dictates a Hindu's life. Hindus believe in the one Supreme Being but whose manifestations are many. The trinity of Brahma, Vishnu and Shiva are all aspects of the one Supreme Being that is worshipped, while karma—action that governs one's life—and reincarnation, i.e. rebirth, are tenets that regulate life.

Hinduism is one of the oldest religions in the world and the third largest in following after Islam and Christianity. Hinduism is at times referred to as Sanatana Dharma or eternal law, and there is complete freedom of belief and worship within the Hindu context. It is said that one has to be born a Hindu and that Hinduism is a way of life. Buddhism, Jainism and even Sikhism are spinoffs. There are about 940 million Hindus living in India. Bali, Bangladesh and Nepal, which used to be a Hindu kingdom, have large Hindu populations. Unlike all other religions it has no single founder.

8   Spreading the Word of God

The sky was dark and eerie. It lit up in brilliant flashes every now and then, while thunder growled ominously in the not so far distance. A heavy downpour appeared to be imminent. Nanak and Mardana knew if they didn't hurry they would soon be caught in the deluge. Not only would they be drenched, they would be without shelter too. For they were on foot and in between villages.

Although our hi-tech airplanes, bullet trains and super cars have made the world a much smaller place, getting from one place to another still takes a lot of time and effort. In the 16th century, with none of these exciting modes of transport, it would have been much worse and almost next to impossible. Yet Guru Nanak managed not only to go to practically every corner of India, but also as far as Sri Lanka, Mecca and Baghdad.

When kings in the medieval ages wished to travel, they were carried in palanquins while warriors rode horses, camels and elephants. But if you were neither of those, how would you travel?

You would walk.

And so did Guru Nanak. On certain days through rain and slush, and on other days with the sun mercilessly beating down upon him. He trekked up mountains and down valleys. Through dust storms and hail. Through floods and searing heat.

And what made him do it? He did it for the common good of man.

The compulsion to try and change a caste-ridden society that was steeped in religious disharmony into a casteless one, with a more harmonious and liberal way of thinking, made him brave the furies of the elements with no thought to himself or his comforts. Like Buddha and Mahavira before him, he too felt he had to spread the word of God throughout the world at any cost. So he left his family and friends, his comforts and home, and set out to do what he felt he needed to do. He believed he had a divine undertaking, he needed to tell people that 'Truth' was all important, but 'Truthful Living' was even more vital. He needed people to know that:

There is only one God.
He is the creator and is without form.
He is Truth.
He is supreme and timeless.
All are equal before Him.
Castes and divisive religions are man-made.
Good and bad, victory and defeat, all happen at God's will.
Rituals and ceremonies are not necessary to please God.
A life lived with tolerance, compassion, devotion and truth pleases God.

Woman, the mother of man, is not in any way
inferior.
There is no need to become a yogi or a sanyasi
to reach God.
Choose a Guru to guide you,
Then
Kirit Karo (Work),
Nam Japo (Meditate)
Vand Karo (Share)
And you will achieve salvation in this world itself.

Guru Nanak's teachings were simple and direct. He
spoke in Punjabi which was the language of the masses.
For the first time the word of God was being explained to
them not in Sanskrit, or in Persian, but in a language they
could understand. The beauty of his words was enhanced
by the manner in which he delivered them. They were
laced with gentle humour. He also composed them
into verses and hymns and with the help of Mardana,
set them to music. He believed that music linked man
to God. He combined what he felt was good in both
Hinduism and Islam, and presented it as a more liberal
school of thought. He became a reformer—a redeemer
in a world that appeared to have lost its way. His disciples
were at first referred to as 'Shishya', meaning disciple,
in Sanskrit till it developed into 'Sikh', and soon his
followers came to be known as Sikhs. And his teachings
or religion 'Sikhism'.

In order to spread his message he undertook four
long journeys. He spent twenty-odd years on the road—

on foot—singing, preaching and explaining his idea of Sat Kartar (true creator) and Sat Nam (true name) who was the one true God.

On his first Udasi—as these journeys came to be known—he went to the east. It lasted thirteen years, after which he came home for a while to meet his family. He covered Panipat, Delhi, Haridwar, Allahabad, Benaras and Assam, and then with a break at Talwandi he went to Pak Pattan, Goindval, Lahore and Kartarpur.

The second Udasi was to the south, as far as Sri Lanka, covering Ayodhya, Puri, Rameswaram, Ujjain and Saurashtra, and lasted two years.

The third one was to the north, to Kashmir, Mount Sumeru (Kailash), Nepal and Tibet. And the final and fourth one was to the west. He covered Afghanistan, Persia, Mecca, Medina and Baghdad. He may have gone further, but we have no concrete proof that he did.

He finally came back home in 1521 and settled down in Kartarpur on the banks of the river Ravi.

On his journeys he met with many learned and knowledgeable men. He met with kings and fakirs, teachers and students. He impressed one and all with the simplicity of his teachings and the word of God. After each meeting he would combine whatever he had imbibed from them with his own thoughts, compose them into poems and hymns and sing them.

He firmly believed that the word 'I' or the ego was responsible for all our ills.

When we want something or say 'I want this' or 'I don't want this' we are exhibiting our selfish nature. We are not thinking of God or anyone else. He felt that this want or quest for things, whether it be wealth, power or even happiness—which is often at the expense of others—is responsible for all our sorrows and miseries.

If we were unselfish and were prepared to share and give, we would become better people and the world would be a better place.

In fact, on his first Udasi, he happened to reach a village where the villagers ridiculed and scorned him. They refused to even feed him. 'May this village flourish and prosper,' he said when he left. But soon after, when leaving another village where he had been welcomed and fed he said, 'May this village be deserted,' a shocked Mardana asked him: 'Why do you bless the village which ridicules us while you wish to disperse those who welcome us?' 'Because,' replied Nanak, 'it is necessary to keep the first lot of villagers in their own village in case they should spread their ill manners and selfishness to others.' So he wished them well within their own boundaries. But 'if the good villagers should scatter and go in different directions they would be able to spread and share their goodness with other people and make them better.'

Such was his logic that whoever heard him could not but marvel at the truth of his words. And in the same spirit if you tell yourself you will not be selfish with your games or books and share them with others, you would have in a small way done what Guru Nanak was telling us to do 500 years ago—and become a better person.

Come hail or snow, rain or shine, Guru Nanak spent close to a quarter of a century walking throughout the world and spreading his message. He was always accompanied by his faithful companion and musician Mardana. Gradually a pattern evolved. Every day they would go a short distance then halt. Soon a crowd would gather around them. This crowd would quickly swell into a congregation. He would sing to them of love, truth, compassion and the Supreme Creator, while Mardana would play his instrument. He would then have them sing along with him. After that he would sit and eat with all of them regardless of caste or religion. His fame soon began to spread far and wide. He came to be acknowledged as a wise man—a Guru who was a messenger of God. And thus he became Guru Nanak: a name that not only spawned a new faith but is today recognized as one of the great religious leaders of the world. Mardana, his singing companion who chose to accompany him, has an equally special place in history.

Buddha and Mahavira

In the 5th and 6th centuries BCE, the world was a deeply troubled place. When Gautama Buddha (567–487 BCE), a prince of Kapilavasthu which is in present-day Nepal, saw the suffering around him, he decided to leave home in an effort to find answers. He wandered around the country before finding enlightenment under a Bodhi tree in Gaya in north India, which led him to found a new religion known as Buddhism. He too denounced the caste system and propounded the eight-fold path or the middle path for a better life. Buddhism spread across south-east Asia and is today among the foremost religions of the world.

Around the same time Vardhaman Mahavira, another young nobleman, propagated a religion based on ahimsa or non-violence. He too left home to find salvation and after many years of wandering, came to the conclusion that it could only be found through self-denial. He believed that enlightenment would only come once the 'jiva' or life is freed.

9   Companion and Friend

Wandering bards were common in medieval times. They generally roamed the countryside singing about the defeats and victories of rulers or the valour of this king or that. They would also therefore go from town to town carrying news. These wandering minstrels, as they came to be known, were very popular in England and Europe. The ballads or narrative songs they composed and sang were an effective mode of conveying powerful messages. So it was in the India of those times as well.

Guru Nanak too adopted this method to spread his message. He believed in the power of music, like many others before him. He felt that it was the right medium to connect man and God, that it could create the right atmosphere and mood to get people together. So he would compose his message and ask Mardana, an exceptional Rabab player, to set it to music. These verses called 'Shabads', meaning divine words, would then be sung in praise of the true creator. Shabads were like Hindu bhajans and were sung in various ragas or tunes at organized kirtans or singing sessions.

Since Mardana was an experienced musician, it was an easy task setting them to music. He was a Muslim and was about ten years older than Guru Nanak. He hailed from a family of entertainers or 'Mirasis' as they were known. Mirasis earned a living by entertaining people and were popular and well liked. As their earnings were meagre, they usually augmented it with other jobs.

In those days since the postal service, as we know it, was non-existent, these wandering musicians also acted as messengers carrying letters to and fro from far-flung villages. As a result they were constantly on the move and it was their music that kept them company. Mardana's father was one of them.

Mardana, brought up in the tradition of the Mirasis, was used to travelling and singing. He was thus the ideal companion for Guru Nanak in his quest to spread the word of God. He had thrown in his lot with Guru Nanak the day he had joined him in Sultanpur so many years ago, and was always willing to turn a tune whenever required.

He sang and played the Rabab beautifully. He also loved Guru Nanak selflessly and would do just about anything for him. Not only did Mardana become one of Guru Nanak's most ardent disciples, he was soon creating his own hymns in tandem with him. So much so that Guru Nanak began including them in his discourses.

Mardana went wherever Guru Nanak went. He braved the cold and the heat along with his Guru and slept alongside him, many a time in the open, without shield or cover. He may not have always understood his Guru and his messages, but was curious and ever willing to learn. His friend and master in his turn was always willing to explain and teach. Guru Nanak, as was his habit, usually explained his messages to Mardana through examples. And there were scores of such examples.

On many an occasion, a hungry Mardana would ask Guru Nanak if he could go in search of food, and ultimately land himself in trouble. And each time Guru Nanak would turn that into an explanation of his beliefs.

On one such occasion, travelling through Assam or Kamrup as it was called then, Mardana went in search of food.

Do you remember reading about the 'Beauty and the Beast' where a prince had been turned into a beast or of the 'Sleeping Beauty' who slept for years due to a curse? All these stories had an element of magic which was sometimes good and many a time not. Witchcraft and black magic appear to be responsible for all those curses and spells. Similarly, even in medieval India, there were many areas where witchcraft and black magic were believed to be practised. Poor Mardana fell a victim to it in Assam.

Despite being warned by Guru Nanak to be careful of strange women, Mardana was unfortunately enticed by a beautiful stranger. A smitten Mardana forgot all about Guru Nanak and his hunger and followed her, only to be turned into a goat like many other fools before him. He had no idea she was an enchantress. When he did not return, Guru Nanak went in search and soon found a goat tied up at the gate. With one look he was able to spot the black magic and break the spell. A shamefaced Mardana soon materialized before him. An equally lovely queen of the sorceresses also appeared. Her name was Nur Shah. She was known to be a sorceress who cast her spell on unwary travellers and ensnared them. Now this queen of sorcery was not prepared to let Guru Nanak get away that easily. She and her companions tried every spell in the book to enslave him. They even tried alluring him with music, gold, silver and precious gems. But Guru Nanak sat through it all, relentless, singing about the creator and how women should be virtuous and true. Finally the queen accepted defeat and gave in. He then spoke to her about the ills of black magic and witchcraft and asked her to give it all up. 'Lead a normal life and become a good human being,' he told her and her companions. Overwhelmed by the power of his words, she did exactly that and fell at his feet. She and her wicked companions promised to become model human beings.

And what does this episode about Mardana and Nur tell us?

It shows us that his unwavering faith in God helped Guru Nanak withstand all kinds of temptations. His strong sense of spirituality protected him from being ensnared, unlike others like Mardana, who realized the folly of his actions.

His message: *No black magic and witchcraft can affect you if you believe in the power of God. Also, do not succumb to unnecessary temptations.*

On yet another hungry foray for food, poor Mardana learned a 'bitter' lesson. It had been a long day.

They had been walking for hours and were nowhere near civilization. Guru Nanak was tired and Mardana as usual was starving. So Guru Nanak told him to go ahead and assuage his hunger with some fruits from the fruit-laden trees around them. 'But,' he said, 'only eat as much as you need. Not more. And do not carry them with you.' But so delicious were the fruits that Mardana in his greed decided to ignore this advice and carry some for a later meal. Strangely, when he ate the fruits later, they tasted bitter and gave him a dreadful stomach ache. He thus realized the truth. *Take only what you need. Do not be greedy.*

Mardana and his love of food, his proclivity to attract trouble and his panic when faced with danger are all now a part of Sikh folklore. In a humorous vein almost all the Janamsakhis highlight Mardana's various escapades through which Guru Nanak spread his numerous teachings. In another instance, Guru Nanak and Mardana were in the middle of a horrendous storm and a plaintive Mardana was sure that he was going to be killed. So he gave into his fear and lay down on the ground crying, 'Farewell life.' A smiling Guru Nanak told him 'to raise his head, tune his Rabab and sing in praise of God and all fear will be dispelled'—which is what happened! *Believe in God and there is no need to be afraid.*

Yet another anecdote tells us about how after a visit to a village, Mardana was given a lot of beautiful gifts and delicious food for his journey. He carried them for a while before realizing that they were too heavy for him. So Guru Nanak asked him whether he needed all or even any of it for his journey. Mardana said no, that in fact it was a burden. So then 'why,' asked Guru Nanak, 'do you need to burden yourself with unnecessary things?' He thereby indicated the futility of burdening ourselves with material things even in the journey of life.

His message: *Possessions don't always bring you happiness. Don't hanker after them.*

Mardana, till the very end of his life, remained true and faithful to his friend and master. He was Guru Nanak's companion and confidante for more than forty-five years. There is some confusion regarding where Mardana died. Some accounts say that after four decades and more with Guru Nanak, Mardana breathed his last in Baghdad and that a simple monument with an inscription had been erected there. But other narratives—which appear to be more authentic—tell us about how he settled down in Kartarpur with Guru Nanak and died there. And since he wanted his spirit to be free and unfettered, he asked not to be buried. So Guru Nanak is supposed to have slipped his body gently into the river Ravi to the music of the hymns and songs he had helped create. Mardana was seventy-five years old and the year 1534. There appears to be no confusion about that.

Rabab

The Rabab is a classical string musical instrument that was popular in the middle ages. There are two types of Rabab: the Kabuli which was popular in Afghanistan, and the Dhrupadi which was used in the subcontinent. Mardana and Guru Nanak used the Dhrupadi Rabab with six silk strings. It had a hooked neck so that it could be hung around the shoulders.

10   No Caste, No Creed

The caste system is not peculiar to India alone. But nowhere else in the world is it as pronounced as it is in India where people are divided along lines which are apparently dictated by the kind of profession they are in or the work they do. Initially, according to the Vedas, the Hindus had four classes or Varnas of people. They were the Brahmins, the Kshatriyas, the Vaisyas and the Sudras. These Varnas over the years were subdivided into further classes or castes and sub-castes. Those who didn't fall into any of these categories were clubbed together as 'Untouchables' or as Gandhiji was to later call them, 'Harijans', meaning children of God.

The word 'caste' is not an Indian word and is apparently derived from the Portuguese word 'Castas' meaning clan or tribe. When the Portuguese came to India, they were perplexed by the social system and its hierarchy. They began referring to the Varnas and its subdivisions as Castas. And this soon developed into 'caste'.

The Brahmins occupied the top rung of the ladder. They were the priestly class and so were supposedly closer to God. They were educated and were mostly priests, teachers and astrologers. They interpreted the ancient holy texts and conducted all religious rituals, marriages and funerals. Without them no social or religious ceremonies could be performed. Hence, because of their knowledge and intellectual prowess, they were deemed to be above all the others.

Next in importance came the Kshatriyas. They were the warriors and the kings. They were naturally more powerful than the Brahmins but were still considered to be lower because the Brahmins, by virtue of their knowledge of the ancient texts, were supposedly intellectually superior. And knowledge was power.

The Vaisyas came next. They were the merchant class. All the traders and businessmen belonged to this class. They were the ones who supplied and rotated all the wealth but were still considered lower than the other two.

Then came the Sudras. They were the cobblers, the carpenters, the hunters and the farmers, among similar others. Since they actually worked with their hands or did what was considered to be menial and dirty work, they were looked down upon by the other three classes. They occupied the last rung. This class, along with those who didn't fall into any categories, was the one that felt and bore the brunt of the caste system. Even their very shadows (of some of them) were considered inauspicious and they were relegated to living their lives outside the city limits.

Initially this social structure was very flexible and fluid. There were many kings who were Brahmins or Vaisyas, and many traders who were Kshatriyas or

Brahmins. There were even traders who were Sudras, but over the centuries these divisions became rigid and unyielding. No inter-caste marriages were allowed nor changes in professions. The son of a Vaisya could not aspire to become a king nor could a Sudra become a trader. This rigidity resulted in an unequal society where some considered themselves superior to the others. The condition of those who were considered inferior, like the Sudras, became pitiable and miserable. They had neither the money nor the power to prevent the Brahmins or the Vaisyas from ill-treating them. The kings naturally listened to their ministers, who were almost always Brahmins. And just because they knew the ancient texts and the rituals, the Brahmin priests began to think that they had some kind of a divine right above the others. They began misusing that right and the ones who suffered were the ones without any rights.

It was this inequality that Buddha and Mahavira in their time had rebelled against. And it was the same discrimination that Guru Nanak was fighting to remove. If some people were inferior to others by birth then why was the manner of birth of a cobbler baby the same as that of a privileged Brahmin, he asked. Babies from both classes and castes came into the world the same way. Even the colour of their blood was the same or, was it milk that ran in the veins of the baby born of a Brahmin mother or were they born in a different manner, he wanted to know.

So it stood to reason that if God was responsible for one, He had to be equally responsible for the other child as well. Therefore it was evident that as far as God was considered the cobbler's or the lowly carpenter's baby was no different from the children born in a Brahmin or Kshatriya family. All were equal and had the right to be treated equally. No one was superior or inferior.

'It is how you live your life and what you do in life that makes one worthy or unworthy, not birth,' he concluded.

So in order to hit out at the rampant caste system prevailing around him, Guru Nanak during his first Udasi ignored the invitation of a wealthy, so-called upper caste, Malik Bhago, and walked into the house of Lalo, a lowly carpenter.

Annoyed that a holy man should ignore his invitation, Bhago asked him, 'Is the food of a low-caste better than that of mine?'

In answer Guru Nanak told him to bring the delicacies cooked by him. He held them in one hand and in the other he held a piece of bread given to him by Lalo. He squeezeed both. Blood dropped down from Bhago's rich sweets while milk flowed smoothly from Lalo's coarse bread. He then asked a stunned Bhago how he had made his money. Wasn't it by imposing heavy taxes and exploiting the poor on behalf of his chieftain? While a humble Lalo, it was well known, had earned his living by honest sweat and hard work.

'That is why your food spills blood while Lalo's brings forth milk,' Guru Nanak told him, 'and that is why I preferred to share his meagre meal rather than your sumptuous one.'

His message: *Rich or poor, high caste or low, the bread earned by an honest living is superior. God blesses those who live a life of hard work and piety regardless of birth. All are equal in his eyes.*

The Vedas

The word Veda means 'knowledge' in Sanskrit and the Vedas are a set of scriptures that all Hindus follow and live by. While who authored them is uncertain, legend has it that it was the great sage Vyasa who compiled them around 1000–1500 BCE during Lord Krishna's sojourn on earth. It is also believed that these were probably sourced straight from the mouth of the Gods or from various eminent rishis or seers of the time to whom God had revealed them. There are four Vedas and they are collectively known as the 'Chaturvedas' and are the main sources of information about the spiritual life and conditions of the Vedic age. They are in order of importance—the Rig-Veda which is the book of mantras, the Sama-Veda which is the book of songs, the Yajurva-Veda which is the book of rituals, and the Atharva-Veda which is the book of spells. Every book of the Vedas consists of four parts structurally and they are: 1) The Samhitas—hymns or mantras (2) The Brahmanas—rituals and duties (3) The Aranyakas—forest texts which discuss theological ideas (4) The Upanishads—containing various philosophical problems and solutions. The Upanishads include the concluding texts of the Vedas which are referred to as the

'Vedanta', meaning 'end of the Vedas'; and they consist of the very essence of all Vedic teaching. The Vedas actually cover all aspects of life including the propagation of the idea of 'Sanatana Dharma' or 'universal religion' which is what Hinduism is based on. They are the earliest literary records of our civilization and have stood the test of time, since to this day a Hindu's life is guided and in general dictated by the principles and philosophies contained in them. Religious and social customs over the centuries and to date have been and are still being regulated by them. Hence the Vedas are considered to be among the most revered sacred books of India.

11 ✍ No Rituals, No Ceremonies

The banks of the river Ganga were crowded. There were priests and pilgrims everywhere. Guru Nanak and his faithful companion Mardana were also among them. They were in Hardwar, one of the holiest places of pilgrimage for the Hindus.

Many of those gathered there were standing knee-deep in the river collecting the holy water from the Ganga in cupped palms and flinging it to the east, in the direction of the sun.

Guru Nanak stood pondering for a while. Then he did the same, but in the opposite direction, turning away from the sun.

'What are you doing?' asked the priests. 'Why are you offering water towards the west?'

'Why are you offering it to the east?' questioned Guru Nanak in turn.

'To quench the thirst of our departed ancestors,' they replied.

'Well then,' said Guru Nanak, 'I'm trying to irrigate my fields in the Punjab which are in the west.'

'How silly you are,' replied the priests. 'Do you really think your water will reach your lands in the west?'

'Well, why not?' queried Guru Nanak politely. 'If yours can reach your ancestors who are dead and gone we know not where, why can't mine reach my fields which are just a few hundred miles away and nearer?'

The priests saw reason and felt stupid. What he said was true, they realized. They saw the emptiness of the ritual that they had been blindly following all this time. Guru Nanak then told them that rituals and ceremonies were not really needed 'if you loved God as the creator, worshiped him with your entire mind and led an unselfish life. That was all that was required to gain God's blessings.'

Prayag, where the three holy rivers of the Ganga, Yamuna and the mythical Saraswati meet, is called the Sangam. Hindus immerse the ashes of their dead in the Sangam and have a dip to ostensibly wash their sins away. It is considered the holiest of spots and at any given time there are hundreds of sadhus and pilgrims submersed in its waters, offering prayer. Guru Nanak, on the other hand, refused to take a dip when asked to do so because, 'Could a mere bath in the holy waters wash away the sins of the heart?' he asked. Everyone realized he was right. What he meant was that cruelty, hatred, spite, dishonesty, hypocrisy and malice that most people exhibit couldn't be washed away with a simple bath. Only a life lived without all these vices would. He had again subtly highlighted the hollowness of this particular ritual.

Later, in another holy town of Varanasi, he was asked why he did not carry 'the saligram' (holy stone) or the Tulsi malas that most holy men wore. He told them that they were empty symbols of faith, and that such symbols were not required if 'you had God in your mind and truth on your tongue.' His words once again struck a chord among those gathered there.

On yet another occasion the priests of Gaya tried to convince him to join them in their ceremonies to appease the spirits of the departed souls. He refused by saying that good deeds in this life were the only things necessary, not rituals or ceremonies to please God or the spirits in this life or the next.

By travelling to places where people gathered to engage in rituals and ceremonies, Guru Nanak, through his words and verses, tried to highlight the emptiness of the practice of blindly following something without really understanding it. He showed them up for what they were and tried to make people realize that an unselfish life filled with good thoughts and right action would please God more than blind adherence to rituals and hollow ceremonies.

Even in Puri, at the famous Jagannath Rath festival where lakhs and lakhs congregate to pull the chariot, Guru Nanak highlighted what he believed to be the hollowness of ceremonies. He declared in the form of a song that when you could have a celestial *arti* of the sky, the sun, the moon, the stars and all the beauty of nature, where was the necessity to appease God with lights and flowers, conch shells and clanging bells, or perfumed incense and silver salvers?

During his second Udasi, he happened to visit the house of one Dhuni Chand in Lahore. Dhuni Chand was in the midst of elaborate preparations for his father's death anniversary. His vast wealth was on display and all the Brahmins in the city had gathered there for a feast that was customary to appease God and the spirit of his father, according to Hindu belief. Guru Nanak watched the hectic activity for a while, then called Dhuni Chand aside and gave him a needle. He asked him to give it back to him when they met in the next life.

Have you ever heard of anybody meeting up with another after one is dead?

So Dhuni Chand was puzzled till wisdom dawned on him. He realized what Guru Nanak was trying to tell him: when one dies, one does not take anything with him to the other world, not even something as small as a needle. Hence, neither the wealth nor the food the Brahmins were being fed would ever reach his father. On the other hand, sharing one's wealth with the needy would benefit everyone. Once again Guru Nanak, by example, had shown the fallacy of blindly following rituals.

He tried to expose the foolishness of superstition as well when he found a Brahmin drawing a circle round his cooking pot while cooking. 'Why do you do so?' enquired Guru Nanak. 'So that no low caste's shadow will fall on it and pollute my food,' replied the Brahmin.

'Just stop for a moment and think. How can anyone's "shadow" pollute anything?' asked Guru Nanak. The Brahmin realized the absurdity of his actions. He had no answer. 'It is all in your mind,' he told the Brahmin. 'Throw such thoughts out and fill them with truth, self-regulation and correct action. Those are the lines that you need to draw with the thought of God in your heart.'

His message: *Superstition and blind faith are impediments to one's growth as a good human being.*

The Rath Yatra of Jagannath Puri

On the shores of the Bay of Bengal in the Indian town of Puri, Orissa, is the ancient temple of Lord Jagannath. He is believed to be the avatar of Vishnu and devotees believe He resides there with His elder brother Bala Bhadra and sister Subhadra. Every summer on an appointed day after noon, the three of them decked out in colourful flowers and accompanied by clanging cymbals, ringing bells, blowing conches and chanting priests go in three enormous chariots or raths pulled by hundreds of devotees in a grand procession to the Gundicha temple—His garden house—two miles away. After a sojourn of nine days there, these beautiful idols of wood return home in a similarly grand style via another temple—their aunt's—Mausi Ma temple.

Considered to be one of the largest Hindu religious festivals in India, its many rituals are of ancient significance and the procession itself is a colourful cacophony of trumpets, drums and enormous crowds. It is a commemoration of the Gods' annual trip to honour Queen Gundicha whose devotion saw the garden temple built, while her husband King Indradyumna is credited with having built their regular abode—the main Puri temple. Even a glimpse of the Lord Jagannath in the chariot is considered to be extremely auspicious and a blessing. So thousands of devotees descend upon Puri every year to participate in the proceedings or help pull the chariots. The three gigantic 43–45 feet-high temple-like wooden chariots in different colours are on twelve to sixteen enormous wheels. Egged on by mammoth crowds of devotees, they are pulled by massive long ropes and take many hours to reach their destination. It is a truly awesome experience and is said to have spawned the English word 'Juggernaut', meaning 'destructive force' from the idea of a Lord Jagannath on huge lumbering wheels that have on occasion accidently crushed devotees. But this Rath Yatra, as glorified in the Puranas, is said to also bestow luck and good fortune on all those who participate.

12 ✑ Miracles at Home

'You don't look like a Hindu or a Muslim. What is your faith?' Guru Nanak was constantly asked wherever he went. And it was true. His clothes were so peculiar that most people couldn't make out what he was. He probably dressed that way for the same reason. He was neither one nor the other. He was a man of God. A God who was universal, immortal and eternal. And he wanted people to realize that. In the caste-ridden society that was prevalent at the time, symbols of identification were important. So he probably decided he needed to create a new image by adopting something totally different. Something which was not wholly Hindu or wholly Muslim.

So he wore what was actually a combination of both kinds. He changed his attire as and when he thought it necessary. His choice of apparel was also perhaps dictated by the weather of the particular region he was visiting.

He generally wore a long kurta, like the kind the Muslim Sufis wore, but in the colour of the type the Hindu sadhus wore—a deep orange. He also sported a broad white cloth belt like Muslim holy fakirs, and a small, flat turban that again resembled the Sufi saints. On his feet he wore wooden sandals like all holy men.

Due to the cold perhaps, on his trip to the north he wore leather but on his journey to the Muslim countries he dressed in blue like the Hajjis. All Muslims are required to go on a Haj or pilgrimage to Mecca in Saudi Arabia at some point in their lives. Once they do, they are known as Hajjis and they are usually dressed in robes of blue. They also carry a staff, a jug and a prayer mat. So did Guru Nanak.

In the twenty-odd years that Guru Nanak was on the road, the Janamsakhis tell us about the numerous ways in which Guru Nanak sought to spread his message. Sometimes through the power of his speech, at other times through the example of his action. And many times by the power of a miracle through prayer.

On a stopover in Delhi, for instance, after a fairly long stay with a Muslim fakir called Majnu on the banks of the river Yamuna, Nanak spent a night at an elephant camp. Unfortunately, that night one of the elephants died. The grief-stricken mahouts began to wail. Guru Nanak admonished them and asked them to pray instead of lamenting. And lo and behold the elephant revived—coming back from the dead as it were. The story of this miracle reached the Sultan who owned the elephant, and he asked Guru Nanak how he did it. 'Living and dying are not in my hands but in God's,' replied Nanak. 'Can prayer also kill him then?' asked the Sultan. 'Perhaps,' replied Guru Nanak. So to test him the Sultan prayed for the elephant to die again, and to his utter dismay it did, but he was unable to revive it again. 'Bring him back to life,' he ordered Guru Nanak. Guru

Nanak refused, saying he didn't have the power to do so. Only God could do so.

Guru Nanak was undoubtedly showing them the power of prayer.

Similarly, travelling through the forests near the town of Pilibhit, Guru Nanak and Mardana came across some unfriendly yogis. They were Nath yogis, followers of a tantric guru, Guru Gorakhnath. It was a cold, drab winter night and the frost lay thick on the trees and the ground. There was not a single place of warmth or shelter anywhere except by a glowing fire around which the Nath yogis were gathered. The yogis, instead of welcoming them, asked them to get lost and refused to let them keep warm by the fire. An unperturbed Guru Nanak simply smiled and began reciting his hymns. Suddenly the inhospitable yogis, much to their shock, saw the dried up tree under which Guru Nanak was sitting sprouting new leaves and tender shoots. They realized then that he was no ordinary sadhu. They gathered around him and, as was becoming a habit now, were soon won over by his words on God and what religion should be about. Guru Nanak reminded them that humility and prayer needed to go hand in hand.

Just before this incident, on another occasion we get yet another glimpse of his powers when Guru Nanak, pointing to the bitter-tasting soap nuts hanging on a tree, asked Mardana, who was as usual dying of hunger, to eat them. A surprised but hungry Mardana expecting them to be sour and acidic very reluctantly put them into his mouth. But to his amazement he found himself biting into the sweetest fruit he had ever tasted. The tree still exists and a Gurdwara—Retha Sahib Gurdwara—near Haldwani marks the spot. It is said its fruits are even today sweeter than most other similar trees.

Likewise, a pebble off the street at Hajipur turned into an exquisite invaluable gem in the hands of Guru Nanak. And Mardana was sent off to buy them some food with it. The person who recognized its value was a scholarly gentleman called Salis Rai, who eventually became one of Guru Nanak's devoted followers.

Can you imagine a bowl of milk turning into a golden one filled with gold mohurs? Nor could the villager who had left the bowl of milk for Guru Nanak. Guru Nanak had been engaged in religious discussions with another holy man, Sheikh Ibrahim, in a place called Pakpattan. And since it was generally the custom to give alms to holy men, the villager had secretly slipped in a few gold mohurs into the milk the night before. But much to his delight and amazement, in the morning he found the bowl filled to the brim with gold mohurs. His kindness had been thus returned manifold in gold.

During his second Udasi Guru Nanak came across a Muslim fakir who was unwell. He decided to halt there with him for the night. The fakir, though happy, was aghast. He was suffering from one of the world's most dreaded diseases called leprosy.

If you've seen the film *Ben-Hur*, you will remember how Ben-Hur's mother and sister who contracted the disease were ill-treated and made to live their lives in caves with others similarly afflicted. This disease in those days was incurable and extremely contagious.

Today of course it is curable, even though it is still dreaded. In medieval times it was considered a fate worse than death, and those who contracted it were ostracized and sent to live outside the city limits and nobody would go near them for fear of getting it.

And here was Guru Nanak, much to the fakir's disbelief, all ready to stay with him.

Guru Nanak looked at him kindly and began composing a special Shabad. As he recited it, the fakir found his debilitating illness dropping away. His deformities gone, he was normal once again.

Another miracle had just been performed through the power of prayer. And these miracles that changed lives did not stop here.

A poor, lame fisherman in Dayalpur was able to walk again by just uttering the Sat Nam or the name of God when Guru Nanak told him to do so, while in Mathura a man who had been born blind was able to see when Guru Nanak sprinkled some water and recited a prayer. To the great interest of the locals, Guru Nanak explained the concept of one God and His universality, whether he is known as Krishna or by any other name.

On yet another occasion, this time in Kartarpur where Guru Nanak eventually settled down, a rich man called Karoria felt threatened by the popularity of Guru Nanak. He thus tried to harm him. But when he set out to do so, his horse refused to go forward. When he tried again, he found himself going blind. Even though everyone around him told him of the divinity of the Guru he wanted to harm, he wasn't prepared to believe them. It was only when he was foiled again and again from reaching Guru Nanak that he realized Guru Nanak's power and divinity. So forgetting all intentions of harming him he decided to just go and meet him, but this time on foot. He was now able to reach him easily. Guru Nanak received him well and blessed him.

Another anecdote throws light on how in Ladakh, a demon who was terrorizing the neighbourhood tried to kill Guru Nanak by hurling a huge stone at him. Guru Nanak embraced the stone to prevent it from hurting him and others who were with him. It has his body's impression on it and as folklore has it, it exists to this day and is known as Pather Sahib.

So it is evident that Guru Nanak through the power of prayer wrought divine manifestations whenever necessary. And whenever there was any kind of danger to his life, his own divinity protected him.

What is Haj?

In Mecca, which is today a part of the Kingdom of Saudi Arabia, stands the Kaaba. The Kaaba is an enormous cube-shaped monument containing a sacred black stone covered in gold-edged black silk. It is for the followers of Islam the 'House of God'. Prophet Abraham, long considered to be the forefather of the Christians and the Muslims (Ibrahim to them), is credited with having built the Kaaba in Mecca with his son Ishmael, as early as 2000 BCE as he wanted to promote the concept of worshipping a single God. Among the descendents of Ishmael, who is recognized as being the ancestor of the Arabs, was Prophet Muhammad the founder of Islam. He designated Mecca as the holy city of Islam and the Kaaba, the direction towards which they would pray. A pilgrimage to Mecca was also ordained as one of the five pillars of Islam that needed to be performed by all true devotees according to certain rites laid down by him. So every Muslim is expected to make at least one trip to Mecca in his lifetime, ideally during the last month of the Islamic calendar. This pilgrimage is known as Haj, and one who has been on the Haj is a Hajji.

13 ☙ Miracles Abroad

It is actually on his travels outside India that we see some more results of the astounding power of Guru Nanak's prayers.

In Mecca, for instance, the Janamsakhis tell us that Guru Nanak after his prayers was found sleeping with his feet towards the Kaaba. The Kaaba as has already been mentioned is a granite building in the shape of a cube. It is covered in black silk and is the single-most sacred site of Islam.

The Muslim priests were naturally angry at Guru Nanak's impudence. 'How dare you,' they asked, 'sleep with your feet towards the Kaaba which is the house of God?' Guru Nanak, continuing to lie the same way, told them to turn his feet in whichever direction they thought God didn't exist. Angry, they lifted his feet and turned them every which way. To their shock they found that whichever way they turned his feet, the Kaaba appeared to turn with them.

'Doesn't this prove that God dwells everywhere?' asked Guru Nanak of a very perplexed and agitated group of Muslim priests who had no idea of the powers of the foreigner in their midst. Then when they gathered round him in astonishment, Guru Nanak enlightened them about the reality of a single universal God and the necessity of leading a good life to reach that God. They began to see his point.

But does God really reside everywhere? If you were to stop and think for a moment, you will see that even though we go to visit God in temples, churches and mosques, there is really no place in the world where He is not present even if we don't actually see Him. Guru Nanak rightly said that God is omnipresent and universal.

After Mecca, which he reached by boat, Guru Nanak proceeded to Medina and then to Baghdad. Here he is supposed to have taken up a house to stay on the outskirts of the city.

When he began to recite prayers which spoke about God's unlimited powers and about the different worlds and skies about which only He knew, the chief Muslim priest of Baghdad was horrified. His religion did not speak of any nether or upper worlds that this foreigner was speaking of. Could he be a fake man of God? The priest challenged him to show him the truth of his words. Guru Nanak without hesitation put his hand on the priest's son's thigh. And in the twinkling of an eye all the worlds that Guru Nanak had been describing appeared before him. The priest was thunderstruck.

In Bhai Gurdas' words, 'Then Pir Dastgir asked him which category of fakir do you belong to and what is your parentage?' To this Mardana is said to have replied, 'He is Nanak who has come into the Kaliyug (the fourth and last stage of the world's existence—a period of mistrust, anarchy and disasters) and he recognizes God and his fakirs as one. He is known in all the directions, besides the earth and the sky.'

During World War I in1918, one Dr Kirpal Singh who was a captain in the Indian Medical Service of the British army came across a building in Baghdad which went by the name of Bahlol. It had a picture of Guru Nanak inside it. The inscriptions on it also confirmed the fact that this could possibly be the place where Guru Nanak had halted. Bahlol was a highly respected Baghdadi religious leader with whom Guru Nanak was supposed to have held discussions. In a corner of the city was a well. The water from the well was sweet and pure, quite unlike the water in the rest of the city of Baghdad. This well was apparently dug after the people of Baghdad complained to Guru Nanak about their lack of drinking water. It is said that there are several disciples of Guru Nanak living in Iraq even today, following Sikh traditions, who bear testimony to this story. But sadly, during the Iraq war in 2003, these shrines were destroyed. However, the Iraqi government appears to be determined to build them again.

Guru Nanak also met many wicked men who were openly hostile to him. And the only way he could thwart their hostility and save himself was by the power of his divinity. He also used the same divinity to convert and change them into becoming better human beings, as for instance the arrogant priest called Wali Kandhari.

Wali Kandhari lived a few miles from the city of Rawalpindi where Guru Nanak and Mardana landed up one day during their travels. As usual a congregation began to gather around Guru Nanak. It soon became a regular affair where kirtans in praise of God were sung every night and prayers recited in communal harmony. Kandhari got to hear about this newcomer's arrival and soon grew annoyed at Guru Nanak's popularity. Near his house, on the hill above, there was a spring which he controlled. The water from the spring irrigated the town. It was used by everyone. A jealous Kandhari saw Guru Nanak's popularity as a threat to himself and to teach the town's people a lesson, decided to block the waters of the spring. When they pleaded with him to unblock it, they were rudely told to get their water from their new guru. The people then went to Guru Nanak for help. When Mardana was sent up as an emissary to ask for the water to be allowed to flow, a furious Wali Sahib told Mardana, 'If your guru is so powerful, let him create a new source of water for you.' When Guru Nanak heard this, he asked the people to pray along with him for a while. He then quietly lifted up a stone. Soon much to the villagers' joy and amazement, from under it gushed out a whole new stream of water. Kandhari, on the other hand, suddenly found his spring drying up. Quivering with rage, he sought to push a huge boulder down at Guru Nanak and his men. As the enormous rock went hurtling down to crush them all to death, Guru Nanak simply turned, raised his arms and stopped it with his hands. The imprint of his palm on the stone is visible to everyone to this day. Kandhari, realizing that this was no ordinary man, threw himself at Guru Nanak's feet and asked for forgiveness. The spot is marked by the Panja Sahib (five fingers) Gurdwara, so called because of the imprint.

Thus Guru Nanak used his powers of divinity and prayer as and when he needed to save lives or help people who needed succour.

Baghdad

Once the seat of the famous caliphs of Abbasid and the Ottoman Turks, Baghdad, the capital of Iraq, was among the most beautiful cities of the middle ages. Founded in 762 CE by Abu Jaffar Al Mansur, the second caliph of Abbasid, it not only emerged as a significant centre of medieval Islamic learning but also flourished as an important Arabic cultural and commercial hub (8th–13th centuries) before it was invaded and brutally destroyed by the Mongols of Iran—one of whom was the terrible Timur the Lame who massacred half its population. Uniquely designed as a circular city on the banks of the river Tigris, it boasted of lovely marble buildings and exquisitely appointed parks and gardens within round walls. With one of the celebrated Seven Wonders of the World—the 'Hanging Gardens of Babylon'—nearby, it was home to the legendary Caliph Haroun Rashid and the setting of the famous *Arabian Nights* tales of Scheherazade as well. It was also among the foremost intellectual cities of its times till its decline under the Mongols (8th–13th centuries) and the Ottoman Turks (16th–20th centuries). Subsequently a part of British Mesopotamia (1920–1932) Baghdad with its now many oil refineries, textile mills and tanneries then became the capital of an independent Kingdom of Iraq under the Hashemite dynasty (1932–1958). The Baath party wrested power after a brutal coup (1963) and the 1970s saw a revival in its fortunes when oil prices boomed. It also has one of the largest zoos in the Middle East, but the animals are sadly dying since yet again it is a city under siege. Iraq-Baghdad was invaded in 2003 by a US–UK coalition army on controversial charges of hiding Weapons of Mass Destruction. No weapons were found, but its unpopular president Saddam Hussein was captured and executed (2006) while the once beautiful city of Baghdad continued to be looted and bombed out of recognition.

14 🌽 The Power of His Words

Guru Nanak did not always need miracles to convert and impress people with the truth of his beliefs. His simple words, which were sung to the music set by Mardana, were many a time more powerful than impressive miracles.

Soon after he had set out on his travels, Guru Nanak chanced upon a man called Sajjan in a village in the south-west of Punjab, which is now in Pakistan. Sajjan, to the unwary, was a kind and generous host during the day. He would lure weary travellers with promises of food, water and refuge. He would then rob and murder them at night. Since none lived to tell his tale, Sajjan flourished in his wicked ways. When Guru Nanak stopped by, Sajjan was delighted. Here was another victim ripe for the plucking, he thought. This traveller, he decided, looked prosperous and had an air about him that only the truly wealthy could have. But unfortunately for him, at nightfall and even through the night he was unable to rob or throttle Guru Nanak, for Guru Nanak spent the entire night singing the praises of a merciful God who would forgive the worst of sinners and allow them to live a better life if they gave up their unholy ways. Sajjan had no chance. The message of the words were so powerfully captivating that he fell at Guru Nanak's feet and confessed. Asking for forgiveness, he agreed to turn over a new leaf. He even gave away his ill-gotten wealth to the poor and turned his house into an ashram where the needy could go for food and shelter.

On yet another similar but horrifying occasion Guru Nanak came across a cannibal named Kauda who was terrorizing central India. Some accounts tell us about how Kauda managed to pounce upon a hungry Mardana who was as usual in search of food. He had almost begun to eat him up when Guru Nanak, arriving at the scene to look for Mardana, was able to stop him with the sheer power of his verses.

Some other narratives, on the other hand, describe the scene where cauldrons full of boiling oil greet Guru Nanak when—on the plea of the people whom Kauda had been terrorizing and eating—he goes with a couple of others to meet Kauda.

Smacking his lips, Kauda was apparently thrilled to see so much food coming his way! He got ready to roast Guru Nanak immediately while Mardana and the others, he decided, he would keep to be fried later. He threw Guru Nanak into the roaring fire that had the oil on a boil and waited in gleeful anticipation. But to his utter shock, an unscathed Guru Nanak walked right out of the burning fire chanting the name of God—Sat Kartar. Untouched by the fire, he went up to Kauda and calmly told him to mend his ways.

An astounded Kauda was so flabbergasted that he froze into immobility. So Guru Nanak sat by the fire and recited the Gurbani or the words of the Guru. How far this dramatic version is true is uncertain, but hearing it, it is said, Kauda and his men gave up their cannibalistic ways and from Kauda the demon he became Kauda the Sikh.

Near a place called Sialkot which is now in Pakistan, Guru Nanak arrived at a town that was in the process of being destroyed by the anger of a Muslim priest. This priest, Shah Hamza, had apparently blessed a childless man named Ganga, who had promised to give him one of any children born to him. But when in due course he became the father of three, he reneged on his promise. An angered Shah Hamza cursed the city and its people and threatened to destroy them. He then went on a month-long fast to realize his curse of destroying the entire city. But Guru Nanak talked to him at length and convinced him that it wasn't right to punish an entire town for the sins of one man. So long as there was even one truthful man living there, he told him, that town needed to survive. The Shah finally accepted the truth of Guru Nanak's point of view and relented.

As he travelled far and wide, Guru Nanak met up with not only man-eating demons and vengeful priests but also with wise kings and good men.

Shivnabha was one such king. He was the king of Ceylon, now known as Sri Lanka. But despite his piety and good heart, he was a troubled man for he had no heir.

Haven't you noticed that instead of counting our

blessings we always find unhappiness with just the one odd thing we don't or can't have? So it was with the king.

Guru Nanak, who spent time with Shivnabha and his queen, told him that he had everything that was good going for him. He was wise. His people loved him and he had a beautiful queen. So instead of brooding over the lack of a son, shouldn't he be finding joy in all the many things he had? asked Nanak. He told them to count their blessing instead of crying over something they had no control over. Guru Nanak then comforted them with a long poem of prayer called *Pransangali* which spoke of the need to be content with what one had and to live a life without wants and wishes. Soon after, the Queen delivered a lovely baby boy.

Near Srinagar, Guru Nanak, according to the Puratan Janamsakhi, met a very learned pandit called Brahma Das. Brahma Das was not only erudite but also a very arrogant man. Since he had mastered all the Sanskrit classics and other holy books, he felt superior to everyone. When he chanced upon Guru Nanak, he didn't take to him at first. In fact he began to make fun of him and his odd clothes.

Guru Nanak bore it for a while, then quietly and politely, as he was wont to do, began speaking of 'Maya' which is all 'illusion' and nothing concrete.

'Does it matter how I dress?' he asked. 'If you were a true man of learning and a true believer of God you will surely know that these things are of no importance and are like illusions. With all your knowledge and learning have you not realized that your purpose in life is to be a messenger of God?' So profound was Guru Nanak's message that the pandit realized he had indeed been guilty of running after material things quite unlike a true man of God.

It was not only within the country that Guru Nanak had a profound effect on learned men, but also abroad. Even among the most die-hard of Muslim clerics Guru Nanak was able to hold his own in a manner that not only impressed but also helped convert them to his way of thinking.

During one of his halts near Baghdad, Guru Nanak was once in a discussion with a Muslim scholar about the merits and demerits of religion and prayer. Here he came across a poor man condemned by the Shariat (Muslim court) to be stoned to death. 'Nothing can be done,' declared the mufti, 'the Shariat has decided.' Guru Nanak reminded the Muslim mufti of the words in the 'Kalima' or Muslim prayer he recited every day which said, 'God is merciful and all forgiving.' He then asked, 'How can you not forgive when your God himself is prepared to do so?' The mufti was struck by the truth of his words and the man was set free.

Then in Baghdad itself, which was the heart of Islamic learning in those days, he and Mardana were attacked by the local Muslim population for venturing to sing sacred verses. They turned out in large numbers to stone the infidels who, as it seemed to them, dared to desecrate their holy land by singing un-Islamic hymns. Guru Nanak, fearless as ever, continued to pray and sing but this time he sang verses from the Koran. He then concluded it with an enthralling call to the Sat Kartar—the divine lord. Mesmerized, the crowd fell back in awe. Hearing the divinity in his voice, the chief religious leader of Baghdad, despite himself, was forced to welcome him. 'Who are you and where do you come from?' he asked and began a discussion on religion. So compelling were Guru Nanak's sermons that many, including Bahlol the highly respected Baghdadi religious leader with whom Guru Nanak had held forth on religious issues, became his devoted followers.

Pransangali

Around the year 1510, during his second Udasi or journey, Guru Nanak went to the south. He is reported to have gone as far as Ceylon—Sri Lanka today—whose wise king Raja Shivnabha was a follower of Shiva. But greatly impressed by Guru Nanak's wisdom, the king invited him to meet his queen and persuaded him to stay. He did for almost two years. It was during this time that Guru Nanak is supposed to have composed 'Pransangali', a beautiful poem in twenty-two verses about the silent palace of God and the ways and means of how to meditate on Him. It also dealt at length on the nature of the body and the soul. Be happy and content with what you have and don't hanker after what you cannot was his message. In 1604, Guru Arjun the fifth Guru, while compiling the Adi Granth Sahib, sent one of his disciples to Sri Lanka to bring the composition home. However, Guru Arjun did not include it in the Granth Sahib because he was not completely sure of the authenticity of the text found there.

15 ❦ Outward Trappings Do Not a Guru Make

Religion lieth not in the patched coat the yogi wears
Not in the ashes on the body.
Religion lieth not in rings in the ears
Not in a shaven head
Nor in the blowing of the conch shell
If thou must the path of true religion see
Among the world's impurities, be of impurities free.

> (From *History of the Sikhs*, vol. I,
> by Khushwant Singh)

During his travels, Guru Nanak met many holy men with whom he held discussions on life and religion. He met many yogis, gurus and siddhas or ascetics who had all renounced the world and were living in mountain caves or in places far away from civilization. They had given up their homes, their families and comforts and adopted a life of complete austerity and piety in order to meditate and think of God. They believed that in order to attain salvation or find God or attain power, one needed to lead a life of penance and renunciation. They were convinced they would not be able to find it at home living the life of a householder. So they wandered the world meditating and enduring many hardships in their quest for the meaning of life and religious wisdom. They did not work and had no money or belongings. They ate when someone was kind enough to feed them or not at all. They slept wherever they could find place or in the open or under bare shelters. They wore saffron clothes or none at all, and usually carried nothing except perhaps their prayer beads.

Guru Nanak found all this disturbing because even as he roamed the world, it was gradually becoming evident to him that one didn't have to go live in caves and mountains or renounce one's normal life to find God. Religion, he discovered, did not necessarily mean giving up the world. One could also find God at home as a family man. Even without shirking one's responsibilities, God, he realized, could be reached in everyday life as well and in fact with more dignity if one lived an unselfish life of love, compassion and charity.

All the discussions and debates he had with later Muslim saints and yogic sadhus during his travels only confirmed what he had discovered in conversation with the ascetics of his childhood—that the yogis and sadhus who wandered around in the service of God were themselves also dependant on the food and money that they had renounced. The only difference was that since they were in search of God, they were prepared to accept it as alms from generous people instead of earning it through a proper livelihood.

'So wouldn't it be more prudent to carry on doing one's duty and earn an honest living even while being engaged in the search or service of God?' he asked.

Neither the opinions of the Bairagi Sadhus near Ayodhya, who believed in renunciation, nor the discussions he had with the siddhas in Kailash Mansarovar about the right way to seek God or all the yogis who came to Kartarpur periodically to debate how to find God could change his mind about the fact that one could also find God at home by living a truthful and unselfish life.

In fact when a group of siddhas or ascetics invited him to attend the Shivratri fair on Mount Achal, he promptly agreed. They believed that he would be unable to make it to the summit on time. This was also a subtle challenge. He was after all in Kartarpur leading the life of a family man, while they were acknowledged men of God.

To their surprise, Guru Nanak was not only there waiting for them when they reached, but he was also found meditating under a tree.

They asked him, 'How can a mere householder hope to attain powers and reach God. Surely only those who are pure can do so?' He told them that even a householder could be 'as pure as the waters of the Ganga,' and reach God if he was able to control all his desires, meditate on God's name and believed in sharing.

Unlike most other men of God, Guru Nanak had

realized that saffron yellow robes or a body smeared with ashes did not ensure an instant passage to heaven. Nor was leaving one's family, or giving up eating, a passport to God.

In other words, every single person born on this earth can only aspire to find God if he or she were unselfish, true and honest.

All his thoughts on the subject appear in the form of a dialogue with holy men in his 'Siddha Gosht'—a group of verses set to music.

As a result of his conviction to serve God even while leading a normal life at home, Guru Nanak decided to settle in Kartarpur in 1521 after he finished his fourth Udasi. He lived the life of a householder with his family till his death in 1539.

Even in the mode of eating he highlighted the foolishness of turning into a vegetarian just to please God. In fact, in Kurukshetra for example, during the auspicious solar eclipse, he cooked deer meat (venison) amidst the devotees assembled there. When the shocked pilgrims decided to take him to task, he asked them whether they were not born of flesh and whether they were not made of flesh, so why then would God who created them be displeased with non-vegetarians?

Wouldn't it be more honest, he asked, if everyone including sadhus and householders tried to reach God by giving up dishonesty, lies, arrogance and selfishness rather than by giving up food instead?

They had no option but to concur because the truth in his words was so evident.

Once again, like everything he did in his life, he lived and showed by example that food, clothes and wealth matter very little in life as far as God is concerned.

He also stressed the need to accept with equanimity the disparities and the dissimilarities that exist among men. For when Mardana asked him why God made some men poor and others rich, he said: 'We may not always understand why God creates these differences but be assured that in the larger scheme of things there will be a purpose behind it. So the same God can create both—Wajid the sheikh who is a rich man and also his servant who massages his legs.'

On another occasion when passing through the town of Multan, which had more priests and learned men than you could count, he subtly demonstrated the fact that everyone has his own place on God's earth. The priests tried to prevent him from entering the town by sending him a glass filled with milk to the brim, thereby implying the town was already filled with holy men and didn't want yet another. He sent it back with another equally subtle message. He floated a petal on top of the milk, indicating that there was space for him as well. In fact his presence would only add to the fragrance, not dislodge anyone there.

His message: *Saint or sinner, rich or poor, everyone has his own place on God's earth.*

Inner qualities work better than outer in the quest for God.

Dukh (suffering) and Sukh (happiness) have to be experienced by every person born. How much or how little is dependant on his actions.

Siddha Gosht

Among the many yogis, saints and gurus that Guru Nanak met on his travels were a group of siddhas or ascetics—the Nath yogis. These yogis had renounced the world and were living in the snow-bound caves of the Himalayas. They believed that in order to attain salvation one needed to give up everything in life and lead a life of renunciation and complete austerity. They also felt that only a strong degree of physical and mental exercise through yogic practices would help them attain certain occult powers or siddhis that would free them or give them 'liberation'. Guru Nanak, as is evident, thought otherwise. Withdrawing from the world and one's family was not the answer, he told them. Why were they begging for food from other hardworking householders? he asked. Living as a householder, earning an honest living by honest work is how one attains liberation and that the path to true enlightenment was through leading a truthful life. True yoga was a meditative recollection of the word of God combined with selfless service to the community, he explained.

These discussions that he had with the yogis are known as the Siddha Gosht. They are in the form of a dialogue (questions and answers) between them and consist of seventy-three exquisite verses of six lines each set to music. They explain 'Gurmat' or the Guru's philosophy. They were included in the Guru Granth Sahib by Guru Arjun the fifth Guru.

16 🦶 Along Comes Babur . . .

Listen oh king, survey the scene. Take a warning from those whom you have defeated. Victory and defeat come from God. Do not forget that he who is victorious today may suffer the fate of the defeated tomorrow if he fails to glorify God. They who ruled yesterday, where are they today?. . . Do not sow the seed of cruelty. He who is cruel himself suffers cruelty.

(From *The Great Humanist Guru Nanak*
by Raja D. Singh and J. Singh)

After their fourth expedition into the world, Guru Nanak and Mardana were finally on their way home. The year was 1520. They decided to break journey at Saidapur to meet up with their old friend Lalo, the carpenter. But Saidapur was in an uproar for an attack was imminent. Babur, a descendant of the terrible Mongol Timur the Lame and the dreadful Chenghis Khan, was making his third attempt to capture Hindustan. His rampaging armies from across the mountains had crossed the river and were destroying the areas they were riding through. Sialkot had fallen with hardly any resistance, and perhaps because of that had escaped destruction. But the people were being subjected to terrible atrocities. Babur had then turned east, it was learnt, and was now heading towards Saidapur even as Guru Nanak and Mardana reached there.

Despite the terrible news of rape and plunder in Sialkot, the people of Saidapur were not prepared to give in without a fight. Every able-bodied man was conscripted and the soldiers of Saidapur, unlike Sialkot, put up a spirited defence. They were able to inflict a lot of causalities on the invading army before they were defeated. In retaliation, Babur's men unleashed a terrible carnage. Blood flowed on the streets of Saidapur and bodies piled up everywhere. Every man, woman and child they could find were put to the sword. The rich and able first, and then the poor and the disabled. No one was spared, not even the fawning merchants of the city or the lovely daughters of the town. The once flourishing and happy town was completely decimated. Those who weren't killed they threw into prison. Hundreds found themselves locked up. Among them were Guru Nanak and Mardana as well.

The terrible invasion had a profound impact on Guru Nanak. But to the world he appeared calm and collected. In jail they were all given chores to do. Guru Nanak too was put to work. He was given the task of grinding the corn. He had to turn the mill till all the corn was ground. But soon, even while carrying out his duties, he began to organize kirtans and prayers. Gradually, the anguish and misery of the prisoners began giving way to a kind of acceptance and solace. His air of divinity and the kindness with which he preached to them spread peace and hope among them. So much so that even the jail authorities began treating him with respect and admiration. Then one day the guards noticed that even as Guru Nanak meditated with his eyes closed, the mill was turning on its own. The news spread. Another warden remembered seeing what he thought was unusual the day Guru Nanak and Mardana were taken prisoners. He recalled that when they had been made to carry heavy loads into the prison, the weight carried itself while they walked by its side!

The story of the miracle reached Babur who was now firmly in control of the city. Babur, unable to contain his curiosity, went to see him. The dignified humility of the Guru and the divinity that appeared to clothe him greatly impressed Babur. In the discussion and debate on God and religion that ensued, Babur was more than convinced with the infallibility of Guru Nanak's words. He promptly asked for forgiveness and in fact appeared to have even touched the Guru's feet in repentance. As reparation he offered Guru Nanak anything he wanted. Guru Nanak asked for the release of all prisoners in the name of God and a restitution of all their rights and properties. Without a murmur, Babur, who was soon to become the first Mughal emperor of India, agreed to do so. Thus did Guru Nanak accomplish the impossible.

But the impact of the cruelty, the suffering and misery in the wake of the invasion was so immense on Guru Nanak that it resulted in the 'Babur Vani', a set of beautiful Shabads he composed in protest. It not only speaks about the brutality of the invasion but also about the conditions that existed before and after.

The Mughals

Zahiruddin Muhammad Babur was the founder of the Mughal Empire in India. In his fifth attempt to capture 'Hindoostan', Babur defeated Ibrahim Lodhi in the first battle of Panipat (1526) and captured Delhi and Agra. This empire was to last 200 years.

Babur was succeeded by his son Humayun. Humayun was a kind man but not as accomplished as his father. He lost part of his empire to the Afghan ruler Sher Shah Suri and had to wait it out for sixteen years until he was able to recapture Delhi once again.

Humayun was followed by his son Akbar who was by far the best Mughal emperor. Hailed as Akbar the Great, he was an able administrator and a just king.

Akbar was succeeded by his son Jehangir. Jehangir was a good man but addicted to opium and alcohol. So Nur Jehan his queen became the real power behind the throne. Jehangir was succeeded by his son Shah Jahan who built the famous Taj Mahal.

Shah Jahan's rule is generally known as the golden age of the Mughals when art and culture flourished. Shah Jahan's son Aurangzeb fought his brothers—even when Shah Jahan was alive—for the throne and imprisoned his father. He ruled till 1707. He was an unkind man and is easily the most unpopular of all Mughal emperors.

After him the Mughal Empire went into a slow decline. For the next 150 years the empire, though technically under the Mughals, was battered and sacked by many external invaders with the British also making considerable inroads into India. The Mughal Empire officially came to an end in 1857 when a few sections of the army chose to unite under a completely powerless Bahadur Shah Zafar II and decided to rebel against the British who were by that time in control of most of India. The British put down the rebellion which though known as the Sepoy Mutiny by the British is today considered to be India's first blow for independence against the British. They deposed Bahadur Shah, sent him into exile in Burma and took over the rest of Delhi. They ruled for another 100 years till India truly became independent in 1947.

17 🌽 And then in Kartarpur

For twenty-odd years Guru Nanak had travelled the world singing and spreading the word of God. He had undertaken four long journeys—Udasis—and mingled with the best and the worst. He had sat with kings and saints, the poor and the afflicted, and in a society that had been troubled by much social turmoil and political strife he had tried to show by example the emptiness of rituals and ceremonies and the irrelevance of caste and creed. He had also spoken at length about the glory of God.

Then in 1521, after his last trip, this time to the west, he chose to finally come home to Kartarpur and settle down permanently. He was actually on his way home when his Saidapur clash with Babur took place.

Now why do you suppose he decided to choose Kartarpur?

During his third Udasi to the north, he had happened to travel through the Majha region of the Punjab which lay between the river Ravi and river Beas. He had been struck by the serenity and peace of the area. He particularly liked the expanse that lay on the banks of the river Ravi. So one of his wealthy disciples, Ajit Randhawa, promptly gifted him the land.

Then Karoria, another wealthy landowner who had at first been hostile and had been humbled by a show of Guru's divinity, seeking to show his remorse gifted him some more. So Guru Nanak decided he would eventually settle down there when his travelling days were done. He chose to call it Kartarpur, meaning seat of God. Karoria had apparently wanted to call it Nanakpur but Guru Nanak declined. Didn't all land really belong to God who is the creator? What could be better than calling it 'Kartarpur'—the land of the Kartar or God? And so Kartarpur it was. With more disciples chipping in with their contributions, the settlement grew and Kartarpur soon became a flourishing little township, known for its spirituality, even in his absence.

His parents Mehta Kalu and Tripta Devi moved there along with his wife Sulakhani and their two sons Sri Chand and Lakshmi Das. Unfortunately, his much-loved sister Nanaki and brother-in-law Jairam did not live long enough to join them, for they had already passed away in Sultanpur just before he had left on his fourth Udasi to the west. He had known that their time had come and had stopped by to be with them when they passed on peacefully.

When Guru Nanak came home for good, his followers were delighted. The first thing he did was to give up his weird outfits and attire himself normally. He began living the life of a family man in the service of his people and God. He had learnt a lot during his travels. He had realized that rather than continuing to wander the world like an ascetic, it was better to go home and let others also benefit from whatever knowledge he had gained. He also realized that tilling and trading were as important as praying. It just needed to be incorporated into one's daily life. This could not be done if one embraced renunciation. In any case, weren't yogis and ascetics also dependant on the householder for sustenance? And if everyone became a sadhu or a yogi who would till the land or produce the food? So he stayed put in Kartarpur venturing out for not more than a day or two at a time. Mardana, his faithful companion, continued to accompany him. Mardana was now a happy man for his family too had moved to Kartarpur. He had missed them sorely during his travels. His son Shehzada was fast becoming an ace Rabab player, just like his father. However, before long Mardana too passed away. In the arms of his beloved Nanak, looking steadfastly into his eyes, Mardana breathed his last peacefully. Shehzada automatically took his place as Guru Nanak's Rabab player.

Kartarpur became popular as a centre of spiritual learning and healing. And Guru Nanak gradually began enforcing a certain religious discipline. Through his compositions and hymns he sought to educate his people of the evils of ignorance, corruption and oppression. Then through a religious routine he tried to sow the seeds for a new way of living. He introduced a number of traditions. With these traditions he was actually helping to create a new religious society that was happy in its service of God and mankind. These traditions were to become the cornerstone of the Sikh religion as we have it now. These Kartarpur practices or traditions started some 500 years ago by Guru Nanak, which included community work, community praying and community eating, continues to be followed in Gurdwaras across the world to this day.

So if you were to visit any Gurdwara in the world, be it in a small village in the Punjab or even in modern New York or London—regardless of your religion or nationality or who you are—you will find a hot meal awaiting you along with some uplifting divine music in praise of God.

Guru Nanak's parents, now witness to the divinity and greatness of their son, realized with pride the truth of Pandit Hardyal's astrological predictions at the time of baby Nanak's birth. For with every passing day the congregations attracted more and more people. Rich, poor or the downtrodden, academics or disciples, Hindu or Muslim, they came in large numbers to hear their son speak. He spoke not only about universal brotherhood and the need to love but also about man-made differences that caused hate and inequality. He also did not believe in idol worship. All those who came could not but be impressed by the logic and truth of Guru Nanak's words on honesty, compassion and truthful living.

As Kartarpur went from strength to strength as a spiritual centre, his fame as an enlightened master spread. His disciples grew manifold. Some like Taru and Buddha were as young as ten and eleven. Among them were also those like Moola Kheer, who followed his teachings to the letter.

In fact there is this story about an incident in Moola Kheer's house. A much respected guest helped himself to some gold jewellery in Moola's house and walked out with it. Unfortunately for him, at the door the stolen jewellery fell out—right in front of Moola. Moola quietly picked them up and gave them back to the shamefaced man. His reason—no true Sikh would steal. His need was perhaps more, and so what was the point in shaming him further?

Guru Nanak's father soon passed away peacefully while a few days later, so did his mother. Fortunately they had both seen their son's rise to eminence in their lifetime.

Due to perhaps all the spirituality that existed around him, his eldest son, much to Guru Nanak's disappointment, became an ascetic and later founded the Udasi sect which is still popular in the Punjab. The younger one Lakshmi Das was too involved in the material ways of the world to be of much use to his father. So while Sulakhani remained as supportive, faithful and loyal as ever, Guru Nanak felt his sons were not capable of carrying on with his teachings. He realized that he needed a successor, someone who believed heart and soul in the traditions that had been introduced at Kartarpur.

The Kartarpur Traditions

A typical day at the ashram in Kartarpur would start at daybreak with a rendition of some of his beautiful compositions from what is called the Japji, which speaks of one God. It was followed by the recitation of the Asa di Var (ballad) in praise of that one God. Guru Nanak would then be open to questions and explanations. After that would come more prayers and singing. Then it would be time for breakfast. Everyone was required to chip in regardless of gender, wealth, caste or religion. While some busied themselves cutting and chopping vegetables, others washed utensils and vessels while some others did the cooking, serving and cleaning. It was all purely voluntary and they did it by turns. These jobs were not considered chores, but tasks in the service of God and mankind. Then they would all sit and eat together, thus signifying that all men are equal in the eyes of God, before each went out to earn his or her daily bread. The same routine was followed for the midday meal as well. At sunset they would all return for yet another session of Sodar or Raheras, meaning evening prayers in remembrance of God, before sitting down together again to dine. After dinner it would be time for the Sohila which were always sung at night before going home to sleep.

These singing sessions came to be known as Kirtans and the community meals Langar, while the congregations to this day are known as Sangats.

18 🌾 To Meet with His Maker

For eighteen years Guru Nanak had led the life of a householder. He was now about seventy years old. His health was gradually failing and he was aware of it. He knew his life was coming to an end. He realized that he needed a successor. He needed to delegate his responsibilities to someone capable of carrying on with his legacy before it was too late.

He had so many devoted and wonderfully disciplined disciples, so you might wonder who did he choose?

Among his many ardent devotees was one Lehna of Khadur. Lehna had once been an ardent Devi worshipper till one day he had stopped to hear Guru Nanak at Kartarpur. After that he had become a staunch Guru Nanak follower. There was nothing Lehna would not do for him. After staying awhile in Kartarpur, he had gone back to Khadur and put into practice all that he had learnt of Guru Nanak's Kartarpur traditions. He worked so much change in Khadur that the villagers began hailing him with great respect. He was gradually becoming a devotee who was worthy of succeeding Guru Nanak. But what actually tipped the scales in his favour was when one day, with no thought to the expensive garments he was wearing, he selflessly carried a load of dirty, dripping grass and fodder for Guru Nanak. This, realized Guru Nanak, was the kind of man who should succeed him. So he sent for him.

Bhai Buddha, another of Nanak's ardent young disciples, escorted Lehna into the presence of Guru Nanak; Bhai Buddha was to live to the ripe old age of 125. He would witness the anointment of the next five Gurus after Guru Nanak and he himself would become the first custodian of the holy book when it was installed in the Harimandir Sahib at Amritsar in 1604.

As soon as Lehna arrived, a frail but firm Guru Nanak stood up. He asked for a coconut and five coins and when that was brought, he placed the coconut with the five coins in front of Lehna. Then as if to dispel all doubts, if any, among the onlookers, he made Bhai Buddha apply an orange 'tikka' or mark on Lehna's forehead, and announced that henceforth he would be known as 'Angad' meaning limb (or a part of himself). Guru Nanak thus proclaimed him his successor and the next Guru. By thus anointing Angad and not any of his sons as his successor, he was once again emphasizing the point that it was not blood or birth that should decide who is worthy, but how one lives one's life.

Bowing before the new Guru, he handed over all his writings—his compositions, hymns and manuscripts. An overwhelmed but grieving Angad received them with great pride and much humility.

A pall of gloom soon descended upon the town that Guru Nanak had made his own. A sense of impending doom hung in the air. Kartarpur's light was fading and every house was feeling its impact. Guru Nanak knew it was only a matter of time before he departed from the world. His work on earth was done and he had chosen his successor as well. It was time for him to meet his maker. So one day, accompanied by his immediate family and disciples, he made his way slowly to the banks of the river. As the sombre procession wound its way towards the river, more and more grieving people joined in. Not only the entire town but people from surrounding towns and villages, it appeared, were intent on going to bid him farewell. While the river swirled along on its merry way, surrounded by this vast grief-stricken congregation, Guru Nanak decided to sit in meditation for a while under an ancient acacia tree.

But no sooner did he sit under it than a miracle occurred. Can you imagine a decaying tree suddenly reviving? Well, that's exactly what happened. The old and dying tree unexpectedly came alive. It burst into lovely new leaves, tender shoots and flowers in bloom. It was so breathtaking in its beauty that a murmur of awe rippled through the crowd. Guru Nanak, meanwhile, continued to sit in meditation.

Then, 'I am feeling a little tired,' he said softly, his eyes running over his people for perhaps what was to be the last time, and laid down slowly. There was a murmur of anguish among the people. When he covered himself with a sheet and closed his eyes, they could not contain their sorrow. So he told them not to weep; 'instead,' he said, 'sing the Sohila—the night-time prayers—for me.'

One can also almost imagine him saying, 'Do not grieve for me. There is great joy in death. Am I not going to meet my beloved master the creator as must everyone?' As the full-throated notes soared high into the sky, at the stroke of his favourite 'Amrit vela' (the time just before dawn), Guru Nanak drew a deep shuddering breath and to the music of the night-time prayer he loved so much, he gently drifted off to eternal sleep.

Guru Nanak's power of divinity, however, did not end there. Despite all his teachings, an unseemly argument broke out over how his body was to be disposed off. The Hindus wanted to cremate him while the Muslims wanted to bury him. It was then decided that some fresh flowers would be placed on both sides of the body and left overnight. Whichever group's bunch remained fresh in the morning, that group could claim him as theirs. But at daybreak both bunches of flowers appeared as fresh as ever! And then to everyone's shock and amazement when the sheet was removed, there was no body to be seen—only another bunch of flowers, or so say the Janamsakhis. So even in death Guru Nanak produced not only a miracle but also highlighted what he had been preaching all along. That all men are equal and that there should be no divisions along the lines of Hindu or Musalman.

Europe during Guru Nanak's time

When Guru Nanak was spreading his faith, exciting things were happening in Europe and the rest of the world as well. In fact about the time he had his enlightenment, Europe was busy discovering India. Vasco da Gama landed in Calicut on the Malabar coast in Kerala for the first time in 1498. This was the beginning of the Portuguese presence in India. They soon controlled this part of the Indian Ocean and spread to Goa, Daman and Diu. Around the same time, Spain's Christopher Columbus was planting the flag in the United States mistaking it for India, and the great discoverer Magellan was travelling around the world for the first time.

The 14th to the 16th centuries also saw Europe breaking away from the practices of the medieval age. It had been a period that was being stifled by rituals and ceremonies of a vengeful God similar to what Guru Nanak was tackling in India. So apart from being an era of geographical discoveries, this period also saw the impact of the Renaissance—rebirth—and the Reformation of the Catholic Church.

From Florence, its birth place, Renaissance, as it spread across Europe, was creating a brand new order in every sphere—from art and culture to church and country. It also ushered in the era of inventions. The invention of the printing press was primarily responsible for the spread of the Reformation in 1517, which was against the stranglehold of the Roman Catholic Church.

England was also emerging out of the doldrums and the era of British navigation had begun. Her golden run was to continue and flourish under Queen Elizabeth I. Soon there would be no part of the world that did not have an English presence. And during Queen Victoria's reign, it peaked to a point in the 19th century when the sun never set on the British Empire—so vast was her empire.

19 After Nanak . . .

Guru Nanak's son Sri Chand was upset that his father had chosen **Guru Angad (1539–1552)** instead of him. So Guru Angad had to first blunt Sri Chand's open hostility before taking on the mantle of the second Guru in real earnest. He had great tact and was also a good organizer. As the devotees kept increasing, he needed more funds to keep the traditions running, especially the Langars. So he opened up more centres and arranged for the coffers to be filled by organizing the collections. He then made copies of all Nanak's hymns and sent them to all the centres. He created the Gurmukhi (meaning, from the mouth of the Guru), a new composite script formed with the alphabets from Guru Nanak's acrostic and other north Indian languages. The Sikhs for the first time now had a script and language of their own. A vegetarian, Guru Angad was also a fitness freak and promoted wrestling as a game. He fixed the first of the month of Baisakh in spring as a day for an annual gathering of all devotees. Thirteen years after he had donned the robes of a Guru, Guru Angad passed away peacefully, but not before he had passed the baton on to Guru Amar Das of Goindwal.

When he was anointed the third Guru, **Guru Amar Das (1552–1574)** was already in his seventies. He was a learned man and was keen on carrying the legacy forward. He did away with the chanting of Sanskrit slokas at births and deaths and replaced them with the hymns of the Gurus. Like Guru Nanak he believed that women were to be treated with respect. So he banned sati and advocated widow remarriages. During his tenure, Goindwal flourished as a spiritual centre. This irked the Brahmins whose followers were dwindling. They complained to Emperor Akbar, but he is said to have been so greatly impressed with the life there that he refused to entertain their complaints. Guru Amar Das was ninety-five when after twenty-two years of stewardship, he passed away. He chose his son-in-law Ram Das to succeed him.

A man of great learning and much humility **Guru Ram Das (1574–1581)** the fourth Guru was also an able administrator. He laid the foundation for the town (Amritsar) which was to become the seat of Sikh religion and moved there from Goindwal. He built a tank near it and encouraged business and prayer around it. He sent missionaries across the country and encouraged more and more people to join them. He also appointed masands or the guru's representative in centres that were far off. Unfortunately, his tenure only lasted seven years. Bhai Buddha, who was still alive, anointed Guru Ram Das' youngest of three sons Arjun as the Guru on his recommendation.

When **Guru Arjun (1581–1606)** became the fifth guru, his brother Prithichand objected. He believed he should have been chosen as he was older. Even though the wisdom of Bhai Buddha and Bhai Gurdas prevailed for the moment, Prithichand was to continue troubling Guru Arjun all through his tenure. Guru Arjun is credited with the completion of the Harimandir Sahib Amritsar that Guru Ram Das had begun to build. But in order to construct it, he needed money. So all Sikhs were asked to contribute a tenth of their income towards it and congregate there on the first of the month of Baisakh for accounts. This formalized what Guru Angad had started many years ago and continues to this day.

With its four open sides and split levels, the Harimandir Sahib was built quite unlike any Hindu temple. The tank was filled with holy water and after the temple was completed, he called it Amritsar. He was also responsible for the Taran Taran, another tank with healing properties nearby. When he found that there were spurious copies of Gurus' compilations floating around, he decided to compile an official one. He then called for compositions across religions. With the help of Bhai Gurdas (Guru Amar Das' nephew who compiled the 39 vars) who wrote it down, Guru Arjun selected all the hymns personally and compiled them along with his five predecessors' verses into the first Granth Sahib. This was the first Adi Granth. It was formally installed in the temple at Amritsar in 1604 and Bhai Buddha was appointed the first Reader or Granthi. It was an embodiment of Guru Nanak's beliefs in its entirety.

Guru Arjun's importance grew in direct proportion to the revenues that poured in and the followers that flocked in. Emperor Akbar's patronage also facilitated the spread of the religion and Guru Arjun's popularity. But after Akbar's death when his son Jehangir came to the throne, he was determined to clip his powers. He felt threatened by the power centre that was gathering around the extremely popular Guru. So when his son Khusrau, who rebelled against him, stopped by to greet the Guru, Jehangir used that as an excuse to persecute the Guru. He imposed a massive fine and when Guru Arjun refused to pay, he sentenced him to death. Jehangir also let loose a reign of terror against all those he thought had supported his son. Many Sikhs were killed, tortured and humiliated, and Guru Arjun was accused of treason. Just before he died, he chose his eleven-year-old son Hargobind as the sixth Guru, and an aging Bhai Buddha anointed him.

Guru Arjun had been Guru for twenty-five years. And in that twenty-five years he had not only carried Guru Nanak's legacy forward, but had formalized the identity of the Sikhs into a separate entity distinct from the Hindus and the Muslims. He had also created a new scripture or holy book that not only embodied Guru Nanak's hymns but also included the best of Hindu and Muslim thoughts. The Sikhs thus, like the Hindus and the Muslims, came to have their own holy book and their own way of living. He had also raised four flourishing towns—Amritsar, Taran Taran, a new Kartarpur and Sri Hargobindpur, named after his son.

Hereditary

When the third Guru, Guru Amar Das, decided to make his son-in-law Ram Das the fourth Guru, it started the trend for the hereditary anointment of Gurus.

Ram Das chose his youngest son Arjun to succeed him as the fifth Guru while Arjun's eleven-year-old son Hargobind became the sixth Guru after him. Hargobind decided on his fourteen-year-old grandson Har Rai (son Gurditta's son) to succeed him as the seventh Guru. And Har Rai chose his five-year-old son Hari Krishen as the eighth guru, ignoring the claims of his elder son. Later this five year old went back a few generations and nominated his grand uncle—great grandfather Hargobind's son, Tegh Bahadur (who was his own grandfather Gurditta's brother)—as the ninth Guru. Then Tegh Bahadur's son Gobind Singh became the tenth Guru.

There is an interesting story regarding how the seat of the Gurus became a family legacy or hereditary. It is said that once when Amar Das' daughter Bibi Bhani saw her father the Guru sitting on a rickety stool that was in danger of toppling over, she thrust her leg forward and balanced it with her toe to prevent it from falling. With the pressure of the stool the toe began to bleed after a while. Guru Amar Das, greatly touched by this, asked her to make a wish. She apparently said, 'Let all the Gurus always be from the family.' Guru Amar Das was dismayed but felt he couldn't go back on his word and granted her the wish. And thus did it come to pass. Her husband Ram Das, an extremely worthy man, became the fourth Guru, and so on.

20   The Legacy Thereafter . . .

Can you imagine an eleven year old leading from the front? Well, that was what happened when **Guru Hargobind (1606–1644)** was made the sixth Guru by his father Guru Arjun. All Sikhs regardless of age rallied around him ready to avenge his father's death.

His saintly father's torturous death at the hands of the Mughals left an everlasting impression on Guru Hargobind. He realized he needed an army and a kingdom strong enough to withstand further such attacks. He took to carrying two swords on his person and exhorted his followers into arming themselves as well. War exercises were conducted side by side with prayers, and training in warfare was now considered as important as religious instruction. Offerings of arms and horses were welcomed and highly appreciated. He built a fortress made of iron and raised the Akal Takht across the Harimandir where military problems and solutions could be thrashed out. Songs and ballads of heroic deeds and bravery were sung there while Harimandir continued to remain a religious temple of peace. Like an emperor he also began sitting on a throne and holding court and going about in a procession under a royal umbrella accompanied by a retinue of armed guards. Yet despite all this, he remained a staunch man of God. Under him his people evolved into a fighting force still steeply rooted in religious traditions.

But when word reached the Mughal court of the increasing clout of the Sikhs, Jehangir had him arrested and thrown into prison in Gwalior. But the piety and demeanour of the young Guru greatly impressed Jehangir who soon released him. So while Jehangir troubled Guru Hargobind no more, his son Shah Jahan, who became the emperor after Jehangir, clashed with him more than once. Each (three) time the Sikhs inflicted massive casualties on the Mughal troops and emerged victorious. With his sons Gurditta and Tegh Bahadur fighting by his side, he managed to keep them at bay and his flock intact. But knowing he wouldn't be able to escape capture for long, he removed himself to the foothills of the Himalayas in Kiratpur. When Gurditta, whom he had been grooming to take over as Guru, died, he decided to anoint Gurditta's fourteen-year-old son and his own grandson Har Rai as the seventh Guru. Guru Hargobind had been a Guru for thirty-eight years.

Guru Har Rai (1644–1661) the seventh Guru was a peace-loving soul. He had seen more than enough bloodshed in his youth, so he decided to move to a village near Sirmur away from Kiratpur hoping that the Mughals would leave them alone once he was not around. He wanted to project the Sikhs as a peace-loving community. He did succeed to a large extent in his mission, for Shah Jahan who had started out as an enemy soon became more benign towards him.

Since he had grown up on the slopes of the Himalayas, his knowledge of the medicinal values of herbs and shrubs was enormous. He soon acquired a reputation as a healer and greatly respected as a Guru. When all else had failed, he was able to successfully treat and bring Shah Jahan's eldest son Dara Shikoh back from the doors of death. But while this earned him the emperor's undying gratitude, it made Aurangzeb, another of Shah Jahan's sons, turn hostile towards him. Aurangzeb wished to succeed his father and anyone helping his brother in any way was an enemy. But Ram Rai, Guru Har Rai's older son, managed to pacify Aurangzeb and convince him that he had nothing to fear from the Sikhs. Emperor Aurangzeb even gifted him some land for a settlement in what is today's Dehradun. Despite this, when Guru Har Rai knew he was dying, he made his younger five-year-old son Hari Krishen the next Guru instead of Ram Rai. He saw in him the promise of a fine pious leader which he felt Ram Rai lacked. Guru Har Rai's tenure had lasted seventeen years.

Guru Hari Krishen (1661–1664) was an infant when he was invested with the powers of the eighth Guru. But in the short time that he was Guru, he not only grew in knowledge and stature but began exhibiting all the qualities of a great master. Aurangzeb had wanted Ram Rai to be anointed Guru so when a furious Ram Rai complained to Aurangzeb on being overlooked by his father, he tried to broker peace between the two brothers and persuade the five year old to give up his claim. Aurangzeb had seen the havoc wreaked by the

Sikhs on his father's forces, so he wanted a pliant Guru at his disposal. He therefore invited the young Guru to his court. Initially hesitant, Hari Krishen went. He stayed with Raja Jai Singh at Bangla Sahib in Delhi. He impressed one and all with his grasp and understanding but made it clear that this was an internal conflict and it would be settled internally. Sadly he died of small pox soon after. But before he died, he named his great-grandfather Hargobind's son—his grand-uncle—Tegh Bahadur who lived in Bekala, the Guru. Guru Hari Krishen had barely been Guru for three years.

Guru Tegh Bahadur's (1664–1675) ascension to the seat as the ninth Guru was fraught with difficulties. There were many claimants for his seat and they did all they could to thwart him. Even the doors of the Harimandir Sahib were slammed shut in his face. So he retired to Anandpur, a settlement near Kiratpur that he built, and began travelling. Wherever he went, his divinity attracted crowds and he was hailed as the true Guru much to the discomfiture of the other claimants. When Aurangzeb began his policy of persecuting all non-Muslims, his followers implored him to come back. The Guru was a brave and courageous man. Hadn't he fought the Mughals with his father as a boy? So he returned. He actively urged his people not to give in and encouraged them to resist forcible conversions. An unhappy Aurangzeb had him arrested on his way to Agra and tried in a Muslim court. He was asked to convert to Islam or face execution. He fearlessly accepted death, chanting the Japji. The Sis Ganj Gurdwara in Chandni

Chowk Delhi marks the place where he was beheaded, and the Rakab Ganj Gurdwara near Parliament House in Delhi is where his body was cremated. He had been martyred after a tenure of eleven years.

Guru Gobind Singh (1675–1708) the tenth Guru was in Anandpur when his father's severed head was brought to him. He was just nine years old. Under the able guidance of his maternal uncle Kripal Singh he assumed charge. He soon became a fearless warrior and a man with a great vision. He was also a great intellectual and poet. The Sikhs were a dispirited lot after the way Guru Tegh Bahadur had been put to death. So Gobind Singh galvanized them into becoming a fighting force once again. And he set about instilling confidence in them. Anandpur was converted into an armed fortress and he built a strong army. He reverted to the practices of his grandfather Guru Hargobind, and martial arts assumed importance once again. Offerings of horses and arms were encouraged and training in warfare was re-introduced. He formed a new order with a core group of brave men called the Khalsa (pure). Since Guru Arjun's Adi Granth had only the teachings of the first five Gurus, Guru Gobind Singh had a new compilation made with the help of a distinguished Sikh, Bhai Mani Singh at Damdama, which included his father Guru Tegh Bahadur's compositions as well. A courageous, newly rejuvenated community, was born again. Thus the Sikhs slowly evolved into a warrior race that was steeped not only in the fundamentals of war but was also steadfast in its devotion to God. Guru Gobind Singh and his brave soldier saints kept his enemies (hill chiefs of the area) and the Mughal army at bay many a time. But soon he himself was wounded by the Nawab of Sirhind Wazir Khan's men, one of his bitter enemies.

When he realized he wasn't going to survive, he called for the Adi Granth Sahib. He placed five coins and a coconut before it. He then went round it thrice, bowed before it and anointed the Adi Granth Sahib as the eleventh Guru. 'Henceforth there shall be no Guru after me,' he proclaimed to his people. 'This holy book shall be your only Guru. Sacred and immortal it is to be followed implicitly.' And so it is till today. He thus created a new Guru for the Sikhs. One who could never be killed. The Adi Granth Sahib now became the **Guru Granth Sahib**.

Soon after, under Banda Singh Bahadur, one of Guru Gobind's able lieutenants, Sirhind was sacked and the Sikhs tried to liberate Punjab from the Mughal Empire. Although these attempts failed, it invoked in the people for the first time a spirit of Punjabi nationalism. Invasions by hordes of Afghans under Ahmed Shah Abdali and others followed. While with each attack the Mughal Empire weakened, it only boosted Punjabi nationalism. Finally the first independent kingdom was realized when Raja Ranjit Singh (1780–1839) established his reign with Lahore as his capital. The golden age of the Punjab (Sikhs) as a strong military power was to follow till the British annexed Punjab to the British Empire (1849).

After independence in 1947, the Punjab was bifurcated with the major part of it going to Pakistan and the smaller eastern portion coming to India.

How the Khalsa was born

In 1699, Guru Gobind Singh asked all the Sikhs to gather in Anandpur on Baisakhi day. Waving a sword he arrived and in ringing tones asked for the head of a brave Sikh. The crowd stood stunned. One Daya Singh came forward. Guru Gobind took him into a closed tent and the sound of the sword crashing down was heard. He then came out with the blood-stained sword in his hand. He looked around and asked for another head. Another man Dharam Singh, equally brave, stepped out from among the silent and horrified crowd. The same routine was followed. Thus five times did he demand five heads. And five times did they hear the crashing sword. Thereafter Guru Gobind opened the tent and much to the amazement of those gathered, brought forth the five men alive.

Now what was the point of the exercise? It was to highlight not only their exceptional courage but also prove that there were those who were willing to die for their Guru. Calling them the Panch Pyares (Beloved Five) he said they would form the core of a new order called the 'Khalsa'. And to the sound of hymns, he proceeded to baptize them with a mixture of sugar and water (Amrit) that had been churned by a double-edged sword. He then announced that all the Sikhs who joined the Khalsa would now sport a single 'Singh', meaning lion, as their last name and the women would be known as 'Kaur' meaning lioness. With that one defining action, he did away with identifying Hindu caste names like Khatris and Mehta that had still been prevalent, and created a new casteless community.

Those who wished to be initiated into the Khalsa had to be baptized. He or she had to take a sip of the Amrit and adopt the five Ks or Kakas—kesh—keep uncut hair, kangha—carry a comb, kara—wear a bangle, kirpan—carry a sword and kacha—wear shorts. A new code of conduct was also introduced. As many as 20,000 men thus got initiated, while the call of the Khalsa's new form of greeting 'Waheguruji ka Khalsa Waheguruji ki fateh' (Khalsa is God's and victory is God's) resounded all over the Punjab.

21 Woman the Mother of Man

In a woman man is conceived,
From a woman he is born,
With a woman he is betrothed and married,
With a woman he contracts friendship.
Why denounce her, the one from whom even kings
are born?
From a woman a woman is born,
None may exist without a woman . . .
(From *Equality of Women in Sikh Ideology and Practice*
by Valerie Kaur)

Imagine a world without women. Would you be born?
Would anyone be born? So a woman, you might say,
is one of the most important creations on earth. Yet
medieval Indian history is replete with stories about the
degrading manner in which women were treated. Any
male—king or serf—treated them the same way—like
objects or possessions to be humiliated or pleased,
depending upon his whim of the moment.

Guru Nanak was born to such a world. A world that
had no place for women. He couldn't understand why
when life itself revolved around every woman, she should

be treated so shabbily. He found that she had no rights, no wealth of her own nor any kind of freedom. It was as if she existed solely for the benefit of man. She first belonged to her father, then to her brother and finally to her husband, if not her son before she died. And God forbid if her husband were to die before her and she is widowed, her fate then was worse than dying.

But actually this was not always the case. Ancient India respected women and protected her. As a matter of fact, according to the Vedas and other such texts, a woman had equal status in the ancient ages. She was well respected and regarded as equal to man in every way. However, her status began to gradually decline over a period of time. It probably began during the days of the 'smritis' (codes) or the period (200 BCE–200 CE) when Manu, one of our first law givers, wrote out the code of social conduct in great detail in his *Manusmriti*. In it women were bound by a set of rules that completely took away their freedom. This probably rose from the fact that physically women were weaker than men.

A woman's status was now formalized, and it continued to decline through the centuries, reaching its lowest point during the various Muslim invasions which wrought havoc on Hindu society. New social traditions for women came into being. The idea may have perhaps been to protect women, but it resulted in women being treated in unimaginably cruel ways. The Purdah system became the norm. Dowries and child marriages became popular. Sati or throwing herself on to her dead husband's pyre was encouraged. Jauhar or mass suicide was conducted—particularly in Rajasthan—when it was certain their men were going to lose the war. And finally widow remarriage was frowned upon and widows were treated as outcastes. Even their shadows were considered impure. The last blow fell when formal education was denied to all girls to keep them subservient. While no woman was allowed to take any decisions even if it was with regard to herself, she would be punished horrendously if she refused to obey orders unquestioningly. Even if her own father, husband or son who usually loved her wanted to treat her differently, the social code that existed then wouldn't allow it. In other words a woman was not given even a quarter of the kind of respect a man had.

Guru Nanak was a witness to the times. So he began questioning the way girls were being treated. 'Isn't a man born from a woman?' was his first query. 'Doesn't he get engaged to her, marry her?' was his next. 'Doesn't she become his best friend, his partner and if she should sadly die, doesn't he seek out another to keep him company?' So when it appears that man cannot do without her in any way then why is man ill-treating her thus, he wanted to know. His hymns thus began stressing the importance of a woman in society.

'She from whom kings are born and gives life to all our future generations' surely deserves better treatment, for would there be any boy or girl born on earth if women did not exist? A very pertinent point, don't you think?

'Dowry,' his hymns say, 'is a worthless display of wealth and ego,' and is of no real use, so abolish it totally. As for the practice of Sati, he believed that men who truly loved their wives would not want their wives to throw themselves on burning pyres nor would the wives want to do so themselves, because 'true love is to live and bear the pain of loss.'

Guru Nanak hoped by singing about it he would be able to make men ponder, realize the truth of his words and change their ways.

He also began to show by example what he meant. He began encouraging the active participation of women in all the activities in Kartarpur. Women sat side by side with men to pray. They ate along with other men in Langars. Men were required to show respect to women just as they would do their elders. Wives, daughters and mothers were encouraged to be treated exactly like husbands, sons and fathers—with love and respect and gratitude, not as inferiors. Since it was a highly patriarchal society, all this was quite revolutionary for that time. But what Guru Nanak started, his successors continued. They not only preached and practised equality, they practically revolutionized the lives of women. Guru Angad's wife Bibi Khivi and daughter Bibi Amro became well known for being active in all community and spiritual fora. Guru Amar Das appointed women to important religious posts in the districts and banned the Purdah. Mata Sahib Kaur stood alongside Guru Gobind to initiate both men and women into the Khalsa, while Mai Bhago, a woman who joined the Khalsa, led her men into battle to help Guru Gobind Singh. Mata Sundari rose to lead the Sikhs after Guru Gobind's death and is part of the glorious history of the Punjab.

Manusmriti

Among the many Dharma Shastras or ancient texts that still influence our lives is the *Manusmriti* or the texts of Manu. Lord Brahma's son Manu codified in the form of a dialogue whatever he had learnt from his father and delivered them to his students, one of whom was the famous sage Brighu, who then proceeded to explain it to his students as the smriti from Manu or teachings of Manu. *Manusmriti* details the creation of the world and then goes on to describe the rules and conduct by which society needs to live by. In its original form it apparently contained at least 1,000 chapters on law, politics and society, but it mainly dealt with the laws of all social classes.

In 1794, William Jones, a British indologist, translated the *Manusmriti* for the first time from Sanskrit into English. He was thrilled. He had stumbled upon one of India's ancient texts that explained the way society functioned in the past. The laws of Manu were legal laws he assumed, but in actuality they were only a code of social norms that explained how society was to conduct itself. It also included a set of norms for women which while it may have been relevant then is now the subject of much criticism. Now, while this was an important discovery and tells us how women needed to be treated, it is in no way a true example of how women should be treated ever.

22   The Story of the Guru Granth Sahib

When Guru Nanak handed over his body of manuscripts to Guru Angad in 1539, even he may not have perhaps realized the extent of its importance and the role it was going to play in the future—that it would form the core of what is going to be worshipped as the Guru Granth Sahib even 500 years later. But happily it has survived the passage of time, although since its inception the Guru Granth Sahib has had in fact quite a chequered history.

Officially it came into being in 1604 when Guru Arjun installed it in the Harimandir temple at Amritsar and called it the Adi Granth. But its birth could actually be said to date back to Guru Angad, the second Guru, about sixty-five years earlier when he for the first time made copies of Guru Nanak's hymns and created a new script called the Gurmukhi from Guru Nanak's acrostic (a poem in which the first letters form a message). This compilation gave it a formalized form.

Then Guru Amar Das and Guru Ram Das did their bit by attempting a compilation of sorts, which included their compositions as well. But with Guru Arjun, the fifth Guru, it gathered momentum. For when Guru Ram Das anointed him, Guru Arjun's elder brother Prithichand not only contested the elevation but also began intriguing and conspiring against him in more ways than one. He also began compiling a collection of all the sacred writings with a mix of his own compositions.

Guru Arjun then decided that a proper anthology of all the genuine sacred hymns or Shabads needed to be brought out officially if only to prevent spurious ones from popping up every now and then. But in order to do that, he needed to get all the genuine writings in hand first. So he sent for every available text. While some were with the families of the previous Gurus like Guru Amar Das' son Mohan, who needed to be persuaded to part with the 'Pothis' (as these collections were called), many others—some of them spurious—were in various Gurdwaras in the far-flung corners of the country. He then called for religious contributions from the various prevailing Hindu and Muslim sects.

Once he had a sizeable collection of verses, he took himself off with Bhai Gurdas to a place called Ramsar, south of Amritsar. He then sifted through them and chose what he thought were the right hymns. With Bhai Gurdas' help he compiled them into the first Adi Granth. It contained compositions of the first five Gurus and many Sufi and Bhakti saints, apart from those of a few others like Mardana. It took five years to write and was installed formally in the newly built Harimandir Sahib. Bhai Buddha (Guru Nanak's disciple) was made its first custodian. Anyone regardless of caste or creed could and can still go and read from it. This, subsequently referred to as the Kartarpur Pothi, is available in the Kartarpur

Gurdwara in its original. It is displayed to the public on Baisakhi day every year.

After he had finished the Adi Granth, Guru Arjun sent it with one Bhai Banno to Lahore. Now Bhai Banno decided to make himself a copy and add a few of his own compositions to it. So although copies of this version also exists even today, it is not considered authentic. It is said to be in Kanpur with his descendants and is known as the Bhai Banno Vali Bir (Volume).

During Guru Hargobind's (sixth Guru's) time, the master copy of the Kartarpur Pothi went missing. It was reportedly stolen by his grandson Dhir Mal—Gurditta's son—who believed it would strengthen his claim to become Guru if he had it in his physical possession. But to his fury, his brother Har Rai was chosen the seventh Guru. Dhir Mal still apparently continued to hang on to it. After Har Rai came Hari Krishen (eighth Guru). He in turn chose Tegh Bahadur, his grand uncle, as the ninth Guru when the time came and it was he who forcibly recovered it some thirty years later from Dhir Mal, but only to return it to him later. It was at one point of time apparently even hidden away in a riverbed!

After his father Guru Tegh Bahadur was beheaded, Gobind Singh became the tenth Guru. But when he asked Dhir Mal for the Adi Granth, Dhir Mal refused and even taunted him saying, 'If you are a Guru then make your own.'

So Guru Gobind Singh reworked the whole compilation with another devotee Bhai Mani Singh—in a place called Damdama—to include his father Tegh Bahadur's compositions as well and at Nanded, just before he was to die, proclaimed that henceforth it would be the only Guru in perpetuity. He followed it up with the ceremonial anointment. The year was 1708. Since then the Guru Granth Sahib, as it is known, ceased to be just a holy book of sacred scriptures or a Pothi. It took the place of a living Guru. It was subsequently lost during the Sikh wars but fortunately copies were made before it went missing.

There are thus three versions of the Guru Granth Sahib—the Kartarpur Vali Bir (Guru Arjun's volume), the Bhai Banno Vali Bir and finally the Damdama Bir. The Damdama Vali Bir (Guru Gobind Singh) is considered the most authentic and is in current use across Gurdwaras today.

The Guru Granth Sahib

The Guru Granth Sahib is an enormous compilation of about 6,000 verse units. It contains compositions of the first five Gurus and the ninth Guru of Sikhism and sixteen Muslim and Hindu saints along with a few other bards like Mardana. Guru Nanak's hymns, 974 in number, set in 19 different ragas form the core.

You might wonder what ragas are and why they were chosen. Ragas are melodies. They are a blend of ascending and descending musical notes from a given music scale. They depict the mood—joy, anger, sorrow—of the verses. There are many ragas. Since music appeals to everyone, medieval poets used it as a means of expressing their thoughts. Guru Nanak too did the same. He sought to speak and spread the message of God through music and the others followed suit.

The Guru Granth Sahib's other main contributors are Guru Arjun with 2,218 verses (30 ragas), Amar Das with 907 (17 ragas), Ram Das with 679 (29 ragas), Tegh Bahadur with 115 (15 ragas) and Angad with 62 verses (10 ragas) each. 31 different ragas in total were used and it is grouped according to the ragas and not in the order of the Gurus, but within the ragas the Gurus come first, followed by the others. There are also about 22 vars or heroic ballads.

It runs to about 1,430 pages and is in Gurmukhi.

It opens with Guru Nanak's 38 Shabads or hymns of the 'Japji' containing the quintessential essence of Sikh philosophy and ideology. It is the only part that is not set to music and begins with the Mul Mantra or root verse which forms the very basis of Sikhism. It states the core belief that there is only one true God and commences with the words 'Ek Onkar', meaning one God. This is recited at dawn followed by the Raheras—evening prayers—and the kirtan Sohila—night-time prayers. Then comes the main body of the compositions arranged according to the 31 ragas. The ragas were carefully chosen to avoid any kind of provocation. It ends with a shlok called Ragmala, which is a part of the Mundavani or the closing section composed by Guru Arjun.

The Guru Granth Sahib is treated like a living Guru. Always wrapped in colourful silk, it is placed on a platform or a stand (Takht or throne) under a canopy with attendants fanning it. If you were to visit a Gurdwara you will be required to remove your shoes, cover your head and bow before it, before placing your offering. When moved, it goes in a procession to the recitation of 'Waheguru' (hail to the Guru) accompanied by five retainers and is carried wrapped and placed in silk on the chief Sikh's head under an equally colourful umbrella with everyone following it as you would follow a king.

All damaged copies or pages wasted while printing are always cremated as you would a human Guru.

23 🖋 Nanak Pearls

This then is the story of Guru Nanak who rose from a little boy, constantly baffling his father, to a God among men—loved and followed by millions across the world. Even today, five centuries after his time, the foundation of the faith he laid is not only as strong as ever but his teachings are also as relevant now as it was then.

Some of his teachings that you could imbibe:
- Sins cannot be washed away by water, only a clean mind can
- Prayer is of no use unless it is accompanied by good deeds
- Money is good only if it is used for the general good
- Truth is important but truthful conduct is even more so
- Nothing is pure if the mind remains impure
- Do not lie because God is truth
- Do not speak ill of others
- God resides in every heart
- Whatever happens, it happens because of Him
- He blesses us all with His light equally
- Be content with what you have

- Let go of your ego
- Let go of greed
- Plant good thoughts in your mind so that they may spread
- Always think of God. He created you. He will protect you

TRIVIA
TREASURY

Turn the pages to discover
more fascinating facts and
tantalizing tidbits of history
about this legendary life
and his world.

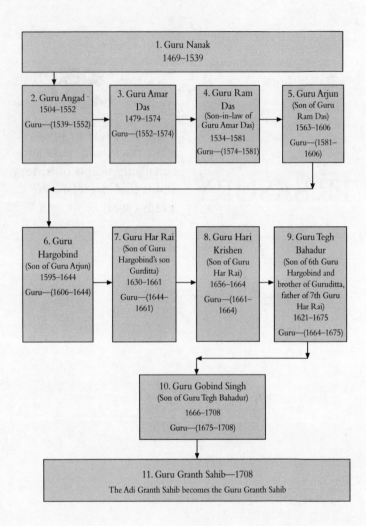

1. Guru Nanak
1469–1539

2. Guru Angad
1504–1552

Guru—(1539–1552)

3. Guru Amar Das
1479–1574

Guru—(1552–1574)

4. Guru Ram Das
(Son-in-law of Guru Amar Das)
1534–1581

Guru—(1574–1581)

5. Guru Arjun
(Son of Guru Ram Das)
1563–1606

Guru—(1581–1606)

6. Guru Hargobind
(Son of Guru Arjun)
1595–1644

Guru—(1606–1644)

7. Guru Har Rai
(Son of Guru Hargobind's son Gurditta)
1630–1661

Guru—(1644–1661)

8. Guru Hari Krishen
(Son of Guru Har Rai)
1656–1664

Guru—(1661–1664)

9. Guru Tegh Bahadur
(Son of 6th Guru Hargobind and brother of Guruditta, father of 7th Guru Har Rai)
1621–1675

Guru—(1664–1675)

10. Guru Gobind Singh
(Son of Guru Tegh Bahadur)
1666–1708

Guru—(1675–1708)

11. Guru Granth Sahib—1708
The Adi Granth Sahib becomes the Guru Granth Sahib

NANAK'S CONTEMPORARIES

- **1499–1547**: Mira Bai, a poetess from the Bhakti era famous for her bhajans on Krishna.
- **1398–1517**: Kabir, a Muslim weaver, whose Dohas represented the Bhakti movement. He lived for 120 years. His verses have been included in the Guru Granth Sahib.
- **1532–1623**: Tulsi Das, the Hindu saint and poet who wrote the Ramcharitmanas.
- **1479–1586**: Sant Surdas, the famous blind poet who composed the 'Sur Sagar' in praise of Krishna.

AND ELSEWHERE IN THE WORLD

- **1450**: Gutenberg invents the printing press
- **1453**: Constantinople (Istanbul) falls to the Ottoman Turks
- **1452**: Leonardo Da Vinci, the great Italian sculptor and painter, is born
- **1492**: Christopher Columbus of Spain discovers the Americas
- **1498**: Vasco da Gama of Portugal lands in Calicut

- **1503**: Pope Julius II is in place in the Vatican
- **1517**: Martin Luther of Germany pastes his demand for Reformation
- **1519**: Ferdinand Magellan of Spain circumnavigates the world
- **1530**: Copernicus discovers that the earth revolves round the sun
- **1531**: Church of England breaks away from Roman Catholic Church
- **1541**: Francisco Orellana discovers the Amazon River
- **1558**: Elizabeth Tudor becomes queen and the English Renaissance is at its peak
- **1564**: William Shakespeare is born
- **1609**: Galileo invents the telescope
- **1680**: Halley's Comet appears

DURING THIS PERIOD …

The kind of food they ate

- Bhaksya (hard), bhojya (soft), chosya (sucked) and lehya (licked) food.
- There were about fifty-six known varieties with thirty-six condiments of food.
- Wheat was staple while maize was unknown.

- Rice was known as tandua and bajra was bajra.
- Payasam or kheer with makuni, a cake made of grams and wheat, were popular.
- Sura and hala were popular alcoholic drinks.

Music they played

- Most of the music we have today saw its birth then.
- Ragas and talas made great strides while Khayals, and Tapas made their emergence.
- Dhrupad style was popular.

Games they played

- Pachisi—A cross and circle board with six–seven cowrie shells. Pachisi, meaning twenty-five, is the largest score that can be thrown to move a player's piece. Played by four it was similar to Ludo.
- Ashta-kashte—A race board game, another form of Pachisi.
- Ganjifa—A card game with horses or elephants on cards. It consisted of twelve sets with twelve cards each. The first card was the king on a horse called ashwapathi/gajapathi. The second was the general's horse/elephant called senapati and then ten other cards with horses or elephants from 1 to 10. Altogether a pack had 144 cards.
- Kreeda Patram—Cloth cards with pictures from the epics were also quite popular.
- All young boys had to wrestle, swim and hunt.

Clothes they wore

- The word sari comes from the Sanskrit word meaning cloth, and was worn in various ways.
- Draped clothing was common.
- Silk saris among the rich and cotton among the poor for women, while men wore loose flowing clothes or dhotis of the same materials.
- Many owned only what they wore.
- When the spinning wheel was invented, handmade clothes gave way to wheel-spun ones and stitched clothing became popular.
- With the Muslims came long tunics and churidars with long scarves for both men and women.

Weapons they used

- Katar—Dagger
- Saif—A double-edged sword
- Nagini Barcha—A snake-like spear
- Karpa Barcha—A hand-shaped spear
- Neza—Lance

Interesting Nuggets

- Arabic and Persian became a part of Indian languages during the medieval ages.
- The Ghazal was introduced for the first time.
- The first Sufi orders were established in India.
- The great Vijayanagara Empire flourished in the south.

- Guru Nanak's original cloak, called the Chola, is said to be preserved in Dera Baba Nanak in Gurdaspur district.
- Guru Gobind Singh's relics can be found in Anandpur Sahib. There is among them a double-edged sword that originally belonged to Prophet Mohammad's grandsons which the Mughal Emperor Bahadur Shah inherited and gave Guru Nanak in return for his help.
- Guru Arjun invited Mian Mir, the Muslim chief priest of Lahore, to lay the foundation of the Harimandir Sahib—the most important of Gurdwara—in Amritsar.
- In 1864 the first printed copy of the Guru Granth Sahib comes out.
- The Harimandir Sahib became the Golden Temple when Maharaja Ranjit Singh had it gold plated in the 19th century.
- The Anglo-Sikh wars were fought between 1845–'49 after which Punjab became a part of the British Empire.
- Large contingents of Sikhs became a part of the British army for the first time.
- The British raised the first Sikh regiments in 1846.
- 300 Sikhs served in the British Indian army during World War II.
- 85,000 Sikh soldiers died in both the world wars together.
- The roots of the present Sikh regiment in the Indian army can be traced to the 11th battalion raised in 1922.

- Today the Sikh regiment is an infantry regiment 19 battalion strong.
- It is one of the most highly decorated regiments of the Indian army. It is also one of the oldest.
- The Sikh festival of Holla Mohalla, meaning mock fight (in March), is celebrated not with colours but with demonstrations of martial arts. It was initiated by Guru Gobind Singh in Anandpur and sees a large gathering of Sikhs even today.
- In 1919, the infamous Jallianwala Massacre took place near Amritsar when General Dyer opened fire on unarmed civilians killing thousands of them. It was a shameful blot on the history of the British Raj. In 1997 when Queen Elizabeth II visited India, she placed a wreathe there in memory of those who had died.
- There are about 25 million Sikhs spread across the world today with Canada and the UK—excluding India—topping the list.

SOME FAMOUS GURDWARAS

Sri Harimandir Sahib (Akal Takht)—Golden Temple (Darbar Sahib), Amritsar—Founded by the fourth Guru Ram Das and built by Guru Arjun, the fifth Guru, it is the most sacred of all Gurdwaras and is central to Sikhism as a religion.

Sri Anandpur Sahib (Keshgarh Takht) Gurdwara, Ropar—Founded in 1665 by Guru Tegh Bahadur, it is where Guru Gobind initiated the Khalsa in Takht Keshgarh Sahib.

Sri Sis Ganj Gurdwara, Delhi—Marks the spot where Guru Tegh Bahadur, the ninth Guru, was beheaded.

Sri Rakab Ganj Gurdwara, Delhi—Marks the spot where Guru Tegh Bahadur was cremated.

Sri Patna Sahib (Takht) Gurdwara, Patna, Bihar—Important as the birth place of Guru Gobind Singh.

Sri Bangla Sahib Gurdwara, Delhi—Built by General Bhagel Singh in 1783 to mark the stay of Guru Hari Krishen, the eighth Guru, in 1664.

Sri Hemkunt Sahib, Uttarakhand—An important pilgrim centre that was discovered by a Sikh, Havaldar Solan Singh. It assumed importance after 1930.

Sri Hazur Abchalnagar Sahib (Sachkhand Takht)

Gurdwara, Nanded, Maharashtra—Built by Maharaja Ranjit Singh in 1839 to mark the site where Guru Gobind Singh died in 1708 after he proclaimed the Guru Granth Sahib as the eleventh Guru.

Sri Damdama Sahib (Takht) Gurdwara, Bhatinda— Where Guru Gobind Singh sought refuge during his battles and scripted the current version of the Guru Granth Sahib.

The five seats/thrones or Takhts where religious decisions are taken are in the Gurdwaras of Golden Temple, Anandpur Sahib, Patna Sahib, Shri Hazur Sahib and the Damdama Sahib.

SOME WORDS OF COMMON USAGE

- *Anand Karaj*: The Sikh wedding ceremony
- *Akali Dal*: The main political party of the Sikhs
- *Akal Takht*: The most important of the five Takhts or the eternal throne in the Golden Temple at Amritsar
- *Nishan Sahib*: The flag of the Gurdwaras
- *Akhand Path*: A continuous—almost forty-eight hour—reading of the Guru Granth Sahib
- *Amritdhari*: One who has been ceremonially inducted into the Khalsa

- *Pahul*: The initiation ceremony of the Khalsa
- *Ardas*: Congregational prayer recited with the daily prayers or just before starting something new
- *Dasam Granth*: A holy book written by the tenth Guru, Guru Gobind Singh
- *Dasvandh*: The one-tenth portion of one's income that is to be donated by every Sikh
- *Granthi*: A reader of the Granth Sahib or someone who is in charge of the Gurdwara
- *Gurbani*: The voice of the Guru or the hymns of the Gurus
- *Gurmukhi*: From the mouth of the Gurus or the written script of the Sikhs
- *Haumai*: Human ego or the 'I' factor
- *Jathedars*: The appointed leaders of the Takhts
- *Naam*: Name of God
- *Simran*: Remembering God through meditation
- *Panth*: The Sikhs as a community
- *Patit*: A Khalsa who does not follow the code of the Khalsa
- *Prakash*: A ceremony before the Guru Granth Sahib is opened every day
- *Sat Sri Akal*: A greeting meaning 'God is true and timeless'
- *Waheguru*: Sikh term for God
- *Gurdwara*: Home of the Guru or the Guru Granth Sahib or their teachings
- *Jo Bhole So Nihal Sat Sri Akal*: The war cry of the Sikh regiment, meaning victory is theirs who speak of the God who is true and eternal

BOOKS TO READ

The books that I have read while writing this:

1. *The Book of Nanak*, Navtej Sarna (Penguin Books India, 2009)
2. *The History of the Sikhs*, vol. I, Khushwant Singh (Oxford University Press, 1999)
3. *The Great Humanist Guru Nanak*, Raja D. Singh and J. Singh (Nirmal Publishers, 1987)
4. *The Philosophy of Nanak*, Ishar Singh (Atlantic Publishers, 1988)
5. *Guru Nanak: His Life and Teachings,* Roopinder Singh (Rupa & Co, 2007)
6. *Guru Nanak,* Harish Dhillon (Indus Source Books, 2008)
7. *Janamsakhi Traditions*, Kirpal Singh (Printwell Publishers, 1966)
8. *The Sikh Religion*, vol. I, M.A. Macauliffe (Oxford University Press, 1909, Internet)

You can also check the link www. Sikhiwiki.org